NORTH SEA

Whiteadder Water

DUNS

BERWICK ON TWEED

TWEEDMOUTH

...lestane Castle

Blackadder Water

HORNCLIFFE

MERSE

RIVER TWEED

Leet Water

Twizel Bridge

The Hirsel

COLDSTREAM

Mellerstain House

Eden Water

Wark Castle

Flodden Field

River Till

...ose ...ey

Smailholm Tower

Floors Castle

NORTHUMBERLAND

...urgh ...ey

RIVER TWEED

KELSO

Kelso Abbey

Bowmont Water

Coupland Castle

Monteviot Park

Kale Water

Lilburn Tower

Teviot

JEDBURGH

Jed Water

CHEVIOT HILLS

THE RIVER TWEED

THE RIVER TWEED

by

JOHN RICHARD THACKRAH

TERENCE DALTON LIMITED
LAVENHAM   .   SUFFOLK
1980

Published by
TERENCE DALTON LIMITED

ISBN 0 900963 98 0

Text photoset in 11/12pt. Baskerville

Printed in Great Britain
THE LAVENHAM PRESS LIMITED
LAVENHAM   .   SUFFOLK

Contents

Index of Illustrations

Acknowledgements

IN WRITING a book of this sort for the general reader it is inevitable that reference has to be made to a great many sources and my debt to the written word is acknowledged in the Bibliography at the end of the volume. Here I wish to record my appreciation of the advice and assistance rendered to me by various individuals and organisations but especially to the Borders Regional Council (Mr A. N. Scott, Tourist Officer, Mr R. Graham, Assistant Tourist Officer and Mr P. Gregory, Assistant Director, Development); the Forestry Commission, Edinburgh (Mr G. Duncan).

Most of the photographs are my own but for the rest I am indebted in varying degrees to Mr Philip Coope, Mrs Maxwell-Scott, O.B.E., *The Liberal News*, the Coldstream Museum (the Curator), and the Scottish Tourist Board (Miss Campbell).

I am also deeply grateful to Lyle and Scott Ltd., for providing me with copious information on the history of textiles, the Hawick hosiery industry and the process of knitwear manufacture, all of which I have relied upon heavily in the chapter on industry.

My sincere thanks are also due to my publishers, for their kindness and help during all the stages of the preparation of this book and I crave the indulgence of my readers for any errors of commission or omission which may have crept into the text and which are mine alone.

Finally and by no means least my gratitude and thanks are due to my parents for reading the draft, passing constructive criticism and for checking the manuscript, typing and assisting in many aspects of research.

JOHN RICHARD THACKRAH

Ilkley,
September 1980

*   *   *   *   *

To my parents

"Whaur sall I enter the Promised Land,
Ower the Sutra or down the Lyne,
Up the side o' the water o' Clyde
Or cross the muirs at the heid o' Tyne,
Or staucherin' on by Crawfordjohn
Yont to the glens whaur Tweed rins wee? —
Its's maitter sma' whaur your road may fa'
Gin it land ye safe in the South Countrie."

John Buchan

CHAPTER ONE

The Scope of the Story

THE story of any river must of necessity give some general indication of the geographical and geological figuration of the countryside through which it flows.

The Tweed in its 97-miles long course from source to mouth flows generally from west to east through the heart of that area of Scotland known as the Borders, an area comprising the shires of Peebles, Selkirk, Roxburgh and Berwick. Geographically and geologically this part of the country forms part of the Scottish Uplands, a dissected plateau of old rock bounded on the north by faults which extend across the country from Girvan to Dunbar. This plateau reaches heights of over 2,000 feet, heights dominated by Broadlaw, Hartfell and Merrick and from which flow the river systems which drain the countryside to the Irish Sea on the west and the North Sea to the east.

The Annan, Liddel and Nith drain the Uplands south-westwards to the Solway and the Clyde carries out the same duties in the north-west. The whole of the eastern part of the Uplands is drained by the Tweed and its many tributaries, the broad lower valley separating the Lammermuir, Moorfoot and Pentland Hills in the north from the Cheviots in the south. The area generally is one of smooth rounded hills, slow moving rivers and few lochs, the hills attaining quite appreciable heights without reaching mountain status.

In the south-east the Cheviots rise to 2,676 feet and Broadlaw in the north-west to 2,723 feet at the junction of the shires of Dumfries, Lanark, Peebles and Selkirk, with the Lammermuirs, Moorfoots and Pentlands forming an arc across the land from near the North Sea coast to mid-country south of the Forth-Clyde valley.

Industrially the basin cannot bear comparison to the Clyde and Forth in the north and the Tyne to the south and most would agree that it is fortunate that this should be the case. However, the industrial revolution has not entirely passed by the Tweed and its tributaries. Here, concentrated in a comparatively small area, is an industry which has sent its products to the far corners of the earth and whose manufacturers are household names in thousands of homes in the five continents. The towns of Peebles, Galashiels, Selkirk, Hawick and Jedburgh, though small in size and population, are nevertheless important centres of employment and collectively form one of the major woollen manufacturing districts in the British Isles, comparable with West

Yorkshire, the West of England, Leicestershire and nearby Ayrshire. Indeed only West Yorkshire can be said to take pride of place and then only in volume of output—certainly not in quality. Hawick is unique in that it claims more foreign exchange than any other town of comparative size in the United Kingdom.

Water-power in nearby East Lothian. *Scottish Tourist Board*

Three factors are responsible for this industrial pre-eminence — old established domestic industries from which traditional weaving skills have been handed down from generation to generation and abundant supplies of wool and soft water. The industrial revolution brought with it water-powered machinery but the area was at a real disadvantage with coal supplies having to be brought from the distant fields of Durham, Northumberland, Lanarkshire and Midlothian. The situation improved dramatically with the introduction of electric power but even so the comparatively sparse population precluded the mass production of ordinary goods and high quality work in blankets, hosiery, tweeds, sports materials and woollens became the speciality of the area and has so remained to the present day. Contrary to what might be supposed the industry does not rely on the indigenous sheep to produce the wool since the local product from Blackface and Cheviot sheep is only suitable for coarse fabrics and carpets and so imported wool is woven into the many fine articles which most people believe are entirely of Scottish origin.

Nevertheless sheep rearing is a considerable economic factor of the Uplands on both sides of the river and its tributaries and the export of the wool to other parts of the British Isles offsets the apparent incongruity of bringing foreign wool into an area already rich in the product. Further down in the valleys there is a high proportion of arable land, that lying below the 250 feet level covering a large extent of the lower reaches of the river basin.

The foundations of the present day prosperity of the farming and woollen industries have their origins going back several centuries to the time when the monks built the abbeys in the middle reaches of the river and had to feed and clothe themselves. To them must be given the credit of founding and establishing sheep farming and after becoming self-sufficient they turned to exporting wool and skins as well as disposing locally of their surplus crops and milk products. These monks and the abbeys they left behind may also be said to have made no mean contribution to the third industry, that of tourism, which has developed at a great pace since the end of the Second World War. The new-found affluence of the population with its increased leisure opportunities and the great advances made in the national and international transport scene have added a new dimension to the economy of the area though the beauties of the river with the salmon fishing and the associations with Sir Walter Scott have also done their part. The catering and hotel trade, country houses and gardens, the functions of the publicity machine and transport are all combining to influence and entice the discerning and discriminating public who want nothing to do with the brash, the superficial and the noisy resorts that are dotted around our coasts like a rash. Those who appreciate and delight in the beauty of the countryside, in romanticism, history, in quietness, solitude and general lack of sophistication will enjoy this

3

area as well or better than most. I hope in the following pages to contribute something towards furthering the interest of those not acquainted with the river and to expanding the horizons of those who are already familiar with its charms and attractions.

Sheep in the Border country.   *Scottish Tourist Board*

CHAPTER TWO

Climate and Geology

CLIMATICALLY there are two principal factors exerting a powerful influence—the shape of the land and the position of Scotland on the face of the planet. Situated in a high northern latitude in a general low pressure area it is subject to the effects of the warming waters of the Gulf Stream and the attendant and prevailing westerly air flow, resulting in a typical Maritime climatic situation. The Gulf Stream ensures considerable wind influence with regular precipitation, though the effects of these are modified to an extent by the attendant equability of temperature which prevents for the most part extremes of cold and heat. The high ground down the western part of the country does affect these general conditions, however, and the southern part of the country with which this book is concerned does have a more Continental climatic condition that the more northerly parts which suffer badly at times from Polar air streams flowing from the Arctic.

Just about every type of weather is experienced at frequent and regular intervals in Scotland—fog, drought, gales, thunderstorms, frosts, blizzards, rain and even sunshine from time to time; none of these phenomena are, however, experienced for any lengthy periods as a general rule, though in the short term they can be very unpleasant and destructive.

The Borders area is further complicated in that its weather conditions are influenced by the continental climate of Western Europe which is only broken in its effects by the sea and by the warm wet conditions moving northwards from subtropical latitudes to the south. This conglomeration of factors ensures the valleys of the Tweed and its tributaries having just about the widest divergence of climatic conditions possible and accounts also for the weather's unpredictability. Rainfall varies considerably from less than 30 inches annually in the coastal belt to over 70 inches on the high ground south of Hawick. The rainfall is unevenly spread throughout the year with the late spring months of May and June frequently being very dry while the early summer months of July and August are the wettest of the combined six months period. The prevailing conditions seem to ensure early springs and mild autumns but if this seems an idyllic situation it must be remembered that the summers are infrequently warm and the winters often severe.

The Tweed region can be divided into two major elements which help to explain the overall topography of southern Scotland.

A wintry sun brightening the landscape at the Loch o' the Lowes. *Scottish Tourist Board*

Firstly, the Cheviot range of hills, dominated by the volcanic mass of the Cheviot, which runs in a north-east south-west direction as do a number of valleys on its north side.

Secondly, the Tweed Basin fringed by the Lammermuir and Moorfoot Hills to the north and north west, and Tweedsmuir to the West. Into this Basin, particularly fertile to the coast, and known as the Merse, run the waters Leader, Gala, Leithen, Whiteadder, Yarrow, Ettrick, Teviot, Jed and Till.

It is clear that in their long life the rocks of Scotland have been subjected to many changes. Later events have obscured the scenic effects of earlier ones, so that most of the features of the present landscape result from geologically recent influences.

In the Border area violent earth movements had the effect of compressing an upward moving strata into a ridge and valley system running north-east south-west. This was followed by subsequent volcanic action when the Cheviot range was formed running in a parallel direction.

It is interesting to delve more into the geology of the Cheviot. All Cheviot igneous rocks, predominantly lava flows, belong to the Lower Old Red Sandstone dating back 400 million years. Volcanic activity began with outbursts of explosive violence mainly along the present Border line, when masses of glowing lava were hurled into the air, accompanied by fragments broken from the internal walls of the volcanoes. This material, known as pyroclast, now forms a deposit some 230 feet or so thick which lies upon the upturned and worn down edges of the Silurian rocks. On the silica-rich, low in calcium, soil abundant heather grows.

After the explosive phase, flows of rhyolite (rich in silica, poor in calcium) poured across deposits of pyroclast—flows which form the high ground today. The main mass of the lava flows is of andesite, which because of the large amount of calcium present inhibits the growth of heather. It is for this reason that the bulk of the Cheviot country is grassland.

Ten million years after the cessation of volcanic activity, a great mass of granite was forced upwards in a molten condition, into the midst of the andesite lavas. This liquid rock melted the lavas around its outer fringe and on re-crystallising formed a rock with a greater resistance to weathering, which can be readily recognised by its darker colour. Granite is poor in calcium and, therefore, like rhyolite lavas it provides a soil on which heather may flourish. The change on the southern fringe of the Tweed basin from high granite to lower lava plateau is accentuated by the change in vegetation from heather to grassland. From any point on the perimeter of the Cheviots the view upwards is one of rolling grass-covered lava hills and deep valleys with the long hump of Cheviot on the skyline.

Additionally, lava flows later broke through the earth's crust to form a series of isolated volcanic hills or laws. Volcanic ashes formed others. Later still, further upward intrusions of basalt rock, known as Kelso traps, created more hills of which the most famous are the Eildons. Such eruptions were responsible for the extraordinarily bumpy landscape, or "basket of eggs" topography, of the Border area generally.

In later volcanic stages, the sandstones of the Carboniferous era were being formed — red in parts of the Tweed valley, such as at Melrose — and in Northumberland the distinctively marked fell sandstone, which at one time was extensively quarried.

Over subsequent millions of years, glacial movement caused further outlayers which lasted until ten thousand years ago. Debris from the Highlands to the Cheviots as well as deposits from the Cheviot itself imposed new land formations on the older rock depositions. Often glacial deposits up to 400 feet thick produced the basis of the region's agricultural economy where good agricultural lands were found in the valley bottoms, terraces and coastal plains. Higher up the valleys moorland vegetation predominated — laid down many thousands of years ago, the foundation of the region's agricultural policy to major primarily on sheep and cattle rearing with more diverse farming on the lower lying lands of the Tweed basin.

The Tweed valley had some influence on the glacier movements, especially as they were related to lines of structural weakness. The Scottish glaciers undertook herculean tasks of transport and deposition, removing vast quantities of rock waste and dumping it elsewhere, for example in Southern Scotland outside the area of heavy glacial erosion.

Another geological aspect is metamorphism which is the true differentiator between Highland and Lowland. Metamorphism denotes a protean change in the nature of the rocks, produced by great temperatures which melt the rocks and, cooling, bring about crystallisation and give birth to such materials as gneiss, granite and schist. They are hard and weather resisting and are Highland features. Where there is a Highland touch in the Lowland landscape, as in the Upper Tweed, it is there because of the presence of metamorphic rocks, but most Lowland heights have weathered to softer profiles. Perhaps more obvious than the absence of rugged outlines is the greenness of so much of this Lowland hill country. This rock is of the Lower Silurian period, sandstones which have weathered away into soil deep enough to maintain sheep pastures and in valleys rich enough to give the fertile lands of Tweeddale once tilled by the monks.

In a progression down the Tweed valley the rocks range from sedimentary (slates, greywacke and hard sandstone) through a small stretch of igneous/volcanic rocks, down to sedimentary with shale and hard sandstone at the estuary. Apart from uplift, folding and faulting, the rocks of this area have been subject to erosion over immense lengths of time, often under climatic and other conditions markedly different from those obtaining today.

Of all the geological features of the Tweed the Eildon Hills are the most spectacular. Millions of years ago the area around Melrose was covered with layer upon layer of consolidated sand and mud. These Silurian rocks were then caught between moving continental plates and pushed together until the mountains were thrown up. Ages of erosion followed until the mountains were nearly flattened and the remains sunk beneath the sea. Then they were covered with a deposit — Old Red Sandstone, that gives the characteristic red soils of the Jedburgh area.

At the end of an active volcanic period Melrose became the centre of a group of volcanoes with the nearest crater centred a mile north west of the Eildons. Not all the molten rock reached the surface as lava and some, after breaking up through the Old Red Sandstone, opened up and filled a dome-shaped layer between the sandstone and overlying deposits. The main mass of the Eildons was formed in this way, not all at once, but by successive intrusions of molten rock.

Rocks over the Eildons were then eroded away, a situation which existed at the time of the Ice Age. Glaciers that covered the area flowed rather north of east and scraped layer upon layer from the rocks over which they passed so that only the very hardest remained. The hard, plutonic rocks are the principal reason for the existence of the Eildon Hills today and are probably only a fraction of their original size.

Another feature is the "tail" of loose rocks deposited in shelter behind the Eildons. Frost action has splintered the rock faces to give the steep scree slopes seen today. Elsewhere the rock has weathered enough to yield a thin soil which is sufficient to support vegetation which much delays any further erosion.

"O Eildon Hills, huge sisters three" from Scott's View.

CHAPTER THREE

Archaeology and Population

SCOTLAND'S prehistory and early history is inevitably geared to the material remains. The earliest historically dated event in southern Scotland and the Tweed valley is the first arrival of the Roman Army in about A.D. 80.

Carbon 14 dating has shown that the beginning of the Neolithic period in Scotland can be dated at about 3500 B.C.

The ice sheets of the Pleistocene period finally retreated from Scotland during the ninth millennium B.C. and left the country open for colonisation by man. During the Mesolithic period the climate altered several times and six thousand years ago the lower parts of Scotland were covered with dense forests. These have slowly been removed by man and replaced by the peat bogs and bare moorland, such a striking feature of the Upper Tweed reaches today.

The early Neolithic period began when the first immigrants, stone-using farmers, arrived in the British Isles by sea from the continent soon after 4200 B.C. bringing with them grain, domestic sheep and cattle. The chambered cairns of this period are the oldest large stone structures in Britain and the earliest of them may have been built not long after the Neolithic colonists arrived; in many cases they were collective tombs.

During the late Bronze and early Iron Age (800-100 B.C.) there is evidence, particularly in southern Scotland, of sites being fortified over a long period, showing how different kinds of defences were in use at different periods. The sequence is often wooden palisaded site; stone-walled fort (not timber-framed); and hillfort with multiple ramparts, introduced to provide defence in depth (probably against the sling).

The appearance of the Roman army in southern Scotland marks an entirely new chapter in Scotland's early history and the siting and design of the Roman field monuments reflect this. These were the works of the highly skilled, professional army of a great urban civilisation penetrating into what appeared to it to be the northernmost limits of the barbarian world. The Roman sites can be understood only in military terms, each fort being linked to the system of roads along which the legions and supplies went. They are planted on flat ground overlooked by hills, in situations which contrast completely with those of the native strongholds.

Sunshine and shadow over the hills of Peeblesshire.

Roman penetration in Scotland went through three stages. In A.D. 80 Governor Agricola occupied southern Scotland, building chains of forts and constructing the main eastern and western roads into the country as at Dere Street. The army withdrew from Scotland in about A.D. 100 because its situation had been made difficult through Agricola's work being unfinished. It returned again in A.D. 140 and built another wall, this time of turf, "after driving out the barbarians". The last phase of Roman activity was early in the third century when Septimus Severus rebuilt Hadrian's Wall, and made repeated forays into Scotland to impress on the tribes the futility of standing against the Imperial army.

Nevertheless, before A.D. 200 the Romans had withdrawn from what is now Scotland and for the next four centuries the lowlands were peopled by two quite different principal races. In the west were the Britons of Strathclyde, whose sway extended from Dumbarton down to Wales, until pressure from eastern tribes cut off the Scottish Britons from the Welsh ones. In the east the powerful Anglian state of Northumbria ended at the Firth of Forth. These Angles might well have pushed the Celts of Strathclyde out of existence and worked their way north until Scotland had become as English as England, but in 685 they were defeated by Brude, King of the Picts, at the great battle

11

of Nechtansmere. Between 843 and 850 the northern tide flowed strongly under Kenneth MacAlpine who united Scots and Picts and the lowlands part of the new Kingdom of Alba.

So by the first millennium A.D. Scotland was inhabited by four distinct peoples, all speaking different languages and two of them recent arrivals. Of these, Scots, Angles, Picts and Britons, it was the Angles, settlers from northern Germany and the Low Countries, who established themselves in north-east England from about the sixth century onwards. They gradually expanded their power, overrunning several small British kingdoms in the process, until in the seventh century they had created the powerful kingdom of Northumbria, the great rival of the Picts. Northumbrian territory eventually included south-east Scotland up to the river Forth and occasionally beyond it. The characteristic Northumbrian decorated stone sculpture is found further north as the influence of the kingdom and of the Roman Church, supported by it, expanded.

It is right on the border with England at Coldstream that some of the earliest documentary evidence exists about Christianity. In 1165 a Cistercian nunnery was founded at Coldstream, one of eleven in Scotland. Nuns were recruited from aristocratic and landed families who gave generously to their foundation and support.

Recent excavations on the site of "The Hirsel" on the outskirts of Coldstream have unearthed some gravestones which could belong to the eleventh and twelfth centuries, such as the ring-headed cross and the plain cross shaft. The cross-marked slabs could be earlier and one remembers that the Tweed valley was christianised by the sub-Roman period. The Tweed basin has been considered a possible early diocese which could have survived from the Roman period to that of the Anglian domination in the late seventh century. When the area came under the jurisdiction of the See of Lindisfarne from the late seventh century the area to the north and south was dominated by important monastic foundations—Jedburgh, Old Melrose, Coldingham and Norham, but these gradually ceased to exist under the Viking depredations of the period from about 870 to 940. The secular control of this area was taken over by the King of the Scots and it would seem that by the mid-eleventh century many parochial churches had been founded by major landowners.

With regard to church buildings, the first major development came to Scotland later in the twelfth century as a result of penetration north of Romanesque architectural ideas (and masons) ultimately from France. Medieval church architecture reached its zenith late in the twelfth century, Melrose Abbey being a good later example, but the confidence of the French architects in achieving great height is not apparent here since the triforium has been omitted to give the church a slightly squat appearance.

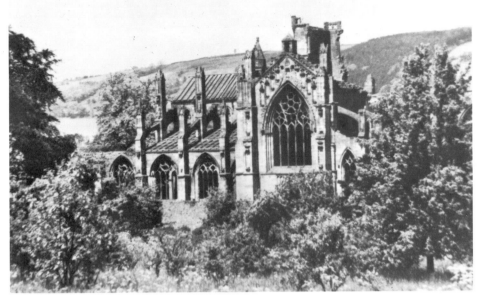

Melrose Abbey.

There are numerous archaeological remains in south-east Scotland, particularly the spectacular ruined abbeys for which the region is famous.

Near Hawick is the stone circle of Burgh Hill, with 25 stones of which 13 still stand — in plan the setting is sub-oval, 54 feet 6 inches south-east to south-west and 44 feet transversely. At Bonchester Bridge is Bonchester Hill, the fortifications consisting of an outer encircling ring of earthworks below the base of the knoll which forms the summit of the hill. There are traces of an inner grass-grown bank.

Moving east into the Cheviots area, the most spectacular site is Dere Street, the Saxon name for the main Roman road. It comes down the gully to the east of Woden Law and there is a good stretch south of this point to Hunthall Hill. The road there is a conspicuous causeway mound, about 27 feet wide and about four feet high. Along the road are the Pennymuir temporary camps, enough to accommodate two legions of five thousand men in tents. Ramparts are well preserved, standing up to about four feet high and being approximately 15 feet thick at base. The nearby hillfort of Woden Law is of considerable interest due to the excellent state of preservation of its rampart and ditches and also because of the Roman siege-works. Just to the north from Tow Ford near Hownam are the rings excavated in 1948, being the first of its kind in southern Scotland to have shown by skilful inter-relation to have been through several periods of occupation. The first phase was a wooden palisade; the second a construction of a stone wall just over 12 feet wide at base, followed by visible banks and ditches round the site consisting of a multivallate system of earthworks to combat long range weapons; the final stage, multiple ramparts, had hardly been completed before falling into ruin.

Since prehistoric times Melrose has been situated at a strategic cross roads. The great Iron Age oppidum of Eildon Hill sits on top of the north of the three hills forming an isolated group overlooking the town. The series of ramparts encircling the slopes around the shallow dome-shaped summit are conspicuous. The oppidum is the largest hillfort in Scotland, enclosing 39 acres. The area consists of a flattish summit with traces of hut circles, a broad plateau below on the south side, and a series of descending terraces running south-west from the top towards the col joining Eildon Hill north with the Middle Hill. In its final phase, the oppidum was a small native town, since 296 circular hut sites have been identified. This is one of the few cities upon hills sheltering inhabitants working on manufacture and industry as well as those tending fields and pastures outside.

At Old Melrose—Mailros of the historian, Bede—an early Christian Celtic monastery was founded between 635 and 650 by St Aidan, monk of Iona and Bishop of Lindisfarne. Close by is a stone chapel dedicated to St Cuthbert who came to Mailros in 651 when Boisit was prior.

In Selkirk one of the few brochs* in south east Scotland is visible at Torwoodlee. It was cleared out in 1891, and excavated in 1950. The circular drystone structure measures nearly 77 feet in overall diameter, the wall being about 17 feet thick, so the diameter of the central court is about 39 feet. Cuttings through the wall of the broch showed that it had been built on top of Roman pottery and glass; most of this was Flavian material belonging to the first Roman occupation of southern Scotland.

In prehistoric times, Peeblesshire was dominated by the pass leading to the Biggar Gap separating the Tweed and Clyde valleys. At Innerleithen an early Christian cross of the ninth century can be seen. At Whiteside Hill is one of the most conspicuous and best preserved hillforts in the Lowlands. Near Stobo, at Dreva Craig, is a rare example of an outer defence formed by chevaux de frise, which is a device to break up a charge of horsemen or chariots, an alternative to rows of pits. One section consists of a hundred upright earthfast boulders with many more fallen or broken and occupies an area 98 feet by nearly 69 feet. Several clusters of hut foundations near Dreva comprise an open village occupied either under the Pax Romana or in later times. At the end of their lives many people were placed in funerary cairns, one of which exists at Drumelzier, where there was a cairn with a kerb, 30 feet in diameter, beneath the centre of which was a cremation pit. Sherds, urns, armlets and a whetstone have been found.

*Prehistoric roofless round tower, with massive walls of unhewn stone.

Just to the north east of Drumelzier lies Tinnis Castle; the oval central enclosure measuring internally 200 feet by 85 feet is defended by a ruinous timber-laced stone wall. Outside this, two more ramparts and several minor defences add strength to the fort. No other timber-laced walls have been recorded in Tweeddale.

At Tamshiel Rig another settlement has features not only unique to Tweeddale but also to northern Britain. It originally consisted of an early Iron Age bivallate enclosure 250 feet by 175 feet, in due course replaced by a walled settlement 140 feet long and 125 feet wide containing several circular stone-walled houses dating from early centuries A.D. These stand at the head of a D-shaped system of fields belonging to a later phase of occupation.

Moving east one finds near Duns the well-known hillfort broch and settlement of Edinshall. This hillfort consists of a double rampart, each line with an external ditch enclosing an oval area 439 feet 8 inches east-west and 239 feet 6 inches in maximum breadth north-south. The final phase of occupation on the site is represented by an open settlement consisting of circular hut foundations in the western half of the hillfort.

One of the rare long cairns in south east Scotland is the Mutiny Stones, north-west of Duns. It is aligned north-east to south-west and is an impressive pile of stones nearly 280 feet long and up to 75 feet 6 inches wide at the broader north east end. Here the cairn stands 8 feet 3 inches high. It has no chamber and may be a northern counterpart of the unchambered long barrows of south and east England.

Relics, generally, of the earliest settlers in Scotland are few and insubstantial. Some of the nomadic squatters gathering their food entirely from natural sources lived in coastal caves and on beaches where their presence has been recognised by the discovery of tools and implements of stone and bone. Others, traced only by mislaid or discarded fragments, sheltered in simple refuges among brushwood and forest trees. Much of the travelling undertaken was by water in the dug-out vessel and skin-covered framework of the coracle type.

After these people came the peasant farmers who soon developed their social organisation and built elaborate and costly tombs. The essence of this mode of living, the woven cloth, the articles of hide and wood and basketry, the ripe grain and the savoury stew have disappeared.

Fresh incursions of people have been traced by new settings, the requirement for which arose from their practising different rites and these have been traced by structural remains and by relics. Late in the third and second millennia B.C. the accumulation of clearances must have produced considerable areas of pasture land associated with arable. Henges,* circles and tall stones were erected for ceremonial purposes and monoliths were on sanctified spots. The homes of people were insubstantial and a continuation of nomadic life was indicated.

---

*Megalithic circular, oval or horse-shoe shaped structure of wood or stone, often surrounded by a bank or ditch.

A cairn.
Scottish Tourist Board

All over the area and in Scotland in general, houses and henges, crannogs*, brochs and hillforts, standing stones, tombs and cairns, though tumbling and decayed, have left a pattern from which a picture can be built up to illustrate developments introduced and superseded as time went by. The rectilinear military works of the Roman armies assert themselves at various strategic points. It is only the erosive action of the plough that has obliterated more of them even farther north. The circular stone houses sprawling over the abandoned walls and ramparts of hillforts and settlements in the southern part of the country bear witness to the years of enforced peace which preceded the final withdrawal of all Roman influence. Earthworks which formed the bases of the defences of the later homestead moats or moated granges still survive in more limited numbers in the southern and central counties. Grass-grown remains of farmsteads of later medieval date, eventually abandoned in favour of more convenient sites, occur in remote places almost everywhere that good land exists. Slopes of many of the hills in the southern part of the country are corrugated with the often striking remains of cultivation terraces or lynchets.

Monuments and the relics contemporary with them provide virtually all the testimony there is of social history of the successive and cumulative peoples who settled and exploited the Scottish countryside through a period extending over some three millennia before records were begun.

*   *   *   *   *

*Ancient Celtic lake-dwelling.

Population trends offer just about as much variety as does the weather and show wide variations when the last century is compared with the present one. In any comparison the effects of the Local Government (Scotland) Act, 1973, implemented in 1975, have to be taken into account. The Act changed the names of two of the counties forming the Borders from Selkirkshire to Ettrick and Lauderdale, and from Peeblesshire to Tweeddale and there were certain demarcation alterations to all of them making exact comparisons impossible. However, it is reasonably accurate to mention that Berwickshire is one of eight counties that have less population in 1971 than they had in 1801 whereas Peeblesshire, Roxburghshire and Selkirkshire are three of twelve counties having slightly more population, Selkirk having in 1971 over twice what it had in 1801. Apart from Selkirk the rest achieved peak population in the nineteenth century and now Selkirk has the highest proportion of its total population residing in urban areas with Roxburgh not far behind. The causes relating to these circumstances can easily be pin-pointed and ascribed to the industrial revolution which led to more mechanisation on farms corresponding with the growth of the textile industry; for the rest the natural desire for greater financial reward and the raising of living standards with its attendant consequence of social ladder climbing were all desirable by-products and natural adjuncts. Even so the Border area has an above average employed population in the primary sector of agriculture, fisheries and forestry.

The following statistics are taken from 1974 and latest estimates for the four Border counties and clearly show the prevailing imbalance between town and country.

	Total population	Area in square miles	Population density per square mile
Berwickshire	17,435	338	51.6
Ettrick and Lauderdale	32,297	523	61.8
Roxburghshire	35,789	595	60.12
Tweeddale	13,584	344	39.5
	99,105	1,800	53.25

		Total population
Coldstream, Berwickshire		1,429
Galashiels	Ettrick	12,788
Selkirk	and	51,628
Melrose	Lauderdale	2,182
Hawick		16,378
Jedburgh	Roxburghshire	3,917
Kelso		4,957
Innerleithen	Tweeddale	2,304
Peebles		6,064

In the case of Berwickshire about a third of the population live in Chirnside, Coldstream, Duns and Eyemouth, the remainder being widely spread on farms and in villages; of the total population approximately 22 per cent are retired persons and these have mostly scattered themselves along a narrow coastal strip.

The population of Ettrick and Lauderdale is heavily concentrated in Galashiels, Melrose and Selkirk which account for some 64 per cent of the total and that of Roxburghshire is similarly centred on three principal towns, Hawick, Jedburgh, and Kelso with the proportion to the total about 6 per cent higher than Ettrick and Lauderdale. About 62 per cent of Tweeddale's inhabitants reside in Innerleithen and Peebles and the county has a higher proportion of retired people than Berwickshire with 23 per cent.

Statistics issued by H.M.S.O. for 1974 emphasise and support the figures of the previous tables. They reflect the changing pattern of hired labour in the twelve years between 1962 and 1974 and illustrate the dramatic decline due principally to the expansion of mechanisation on the farms, the drift from the land to the attractions, if that they be, of work in the factories and mills of the towns, to an exodus from the area altogether in search of more lucrative employment.

	1962	1974
Full time male	4,761	2,826
Full time female	224	134
Part time and casual	885	588
	5,870	3,548

The busy centre of Peebles.

CHAPTER FOUR

Industry

REFERENCE has already been made in Chapter One to the main industry of the Border region but it is of interest to go into its historical background in a little more detail and to give some indication of present day processes.

Historically the textile industry can be traced back as far as Palaeolithic times for it is known that by then early man knew how to twist cord and was conversant with plaiting and sewing. Bone implements, such as awls and needles, have frequently been found during excavations of prehistoric sites, many with cording evidence on them. The lake dwellings of Neolithic man have provided evidence of flax cultivation in the form of thread and cloth remnants; crude implements, such as spindles, spinning whorls and weavers' weights provide confirmation of how the raw flax was processed into crude but serviceable garments. By the late Stone Age the art of spinning and weaving had been acquired in some degree removed from the barely rudimentary. By the time of the first period of Egyptian civilisation, circa 8000 B.C., spinning and weaving were commonplace and there is ample evidence all through the centuries preceding the birth of Christ of many civilizations utilising clothing and furnishings derived from these basic processes.

Sculptures, carvings and paintings show a diversity of apparel of the Chinese, Babylonian, Assyrian, Egyptian, Greek and Roman civilizations — robes, mantles, cloaks, dresses, kilts, skirts, tunics and togas made from silk, linen, cotton and wool. Many references are made in the Old Testament, even as early as the book of Genesis, to a variety of garments made by the principles of spinning and weaving. Even in those early years colouration by methods of natural dyeing had become established and decoration with lace and embroidery ultimately became quite commonplace. Rugs, carpets, awnings and tapestries were made to furnish and decorate the establishments of the nobility. Many written accounts, in addition to the visual, have come down through the ages by such writers as Homer, Herodotus, Aristotle, Ovid and Pliny of the manufacture and usages of silk, cotton, linen and wool.

By A.D. 80 the Romans had established a woollen weaving factory at Winchester and in 901 it was recorded that on Edward the Elder's accession to the throne he "sette his sonnes to schole and his daughter he sette to wool worke". It was, however, the Flemish who laid the firm foundations of the industry that today plays such an important part in the British economy and especially that of the Borders. They followed in the wake of William the Conqueror in 1068, the first weavers' guild was formed twelve years later and in 1107 a colony of Flemish weavers settled in Norwich. From that time onwards there was steady progression for the protection of the industry by a succession of monarchs and parliaments, and processing developments and refinements following the invention of new machinery and the harnessing of power. In 1258 the export of wool was prohibited in order to afford the industry protection from possible lack of raw material. Some seventy years later Jack of Newbury began the manufacture of broadcloth which in a few years became centred on Bristol. The fourteenth century is notable for incidents and occasions concerning woollen manufacture and Edward III certainly did his part in assisting the industry to establish itself. In 1331 a family of seventy Walloons, all of them weavers, came to England under his royal protection and six years later he approved various laws to safeguard the well-being of the industry. In 1350 his parliament approved an Act specifying all kinds and qualities of woollen cloths to be made, in 1368 came the incorporation of the London weavers and a year before his death in 1377 woollen cloth manufacture started in Ireland.

By 1390 the process had spread to the north of England with the recording of coarse cloth weaving being carried out at Kendal. Further safeguards to the growing industry were passed by Edward IV's parliament in 1463 which prohibited the importation of 75 woollen articles, and by Richard III's parliament twenty years later which increased the list of prohibited articles. In 1488 Henry VII's parliament approved an Act forbidding the export of undressed cloths. Politics and religion entered the reckoning in 1549 when Edward VI offered the protestant Flemish weavers refuge from the persecution in the Low Countries by Philip of Spain. Fustian was first made in 1554 at Norwich and when Queen Elizabeth I visited the city twenty-five years later the local children gave her a demonstration of spinning worsted yarn and the knitting of hose. The dyeing of wool before spinning is first recorded as being practised in this country in 1614 and in 1641 Irish spinners exported yarn to Manchester for weaving.

At the time of the Commonwealth the framework knitters of London were granted a charter of incorporation by Oliver Cromwell and this was renewed on the restoration of the monarchy. In 1666 Charles II assented to an act that decreed that all persons, whatever their rank, should be buried in woollens; the purpose was, of course, to expand the woollen trade and came at the fortuitous time of the great plague and fire of London.

Nearly seventy thousand Huguenot refugees from France settled in Britain in 1685 and as many were textile workers the woollen industry received a considerable boost. Two years later a charter was granted to Irish framework knitters. In 1700 the wearing of cotton garments was prohibited in England and this was reinforced in 1721 when fines of £5 were imposed on the wearer and £20 on the vendor of such garments.

To back up all these regulations designed for the protection and promotion of the expanding industry there was the inventive genius of many men. Some of their inventions were comparatively small and insignificant in themselves but all contributed in a greater or lesser degree to the sophisticated production methods in use today. These inventions led to various outbreaks of violence and riotous behaviour by workers afraid of the effects of mechanisation on their livelihood. The best known of these outbreaks occurred between 1811 and 1816 when the Luddites, the name derived from one of their number, an idiot named Lud, wrecked a large number of textile machines in Lancashire, Yorkshire and the North Midlands but others occurred in 1710, 1773, 1780, and 1788; this despite an Act passed in 1727 making machine wrecking a capital offence. Many of those caught and found guilty were indeed executed while others suffered transportation to the penal colonies of Australia.

The woollen and hosiery industry in the Borders was established initially because of the geographical factors of abundant water supply from the Tweed and its tributaries and the accessibility of raw material from the backs of the Cheviot sheep. Nowadays these factors have not the same importance due to the use of modern water purification methods and the ease of importation of raw materials. The manufacture of woollen articles so far as Hawick is concerned is first recorded in 1640 though these were hand-knitted in spite of a knitting frame having been invented in 1589 by the Reverend William Lee of Calverton in Nottinghamshire. The story goes that his wife was knitting him a pair of socks and was taking so long about it that he decided to try to develop a quicker method of production. Eventually he succeeded and applied to Queen Elizabeth I for a patent for his device which was refused on the grounds that it would bring about the ruin of those of her subjects who relied on hand-knitting for a living. This naturally annoyed the worthy vicar who considered that his invention would aid employment rather than further unemployment, so he sought and obtained the patronage of Henry IV of France. It was not until 1605 that the machine returned to England and then only because it was brought back by refugees fleeing from religious persecution. It was, however, 1771 before machines were brought to Hawick by Baillie John Hardie.

Hardie installed four knitting machines or frames which produced worsted and linen stockings for the next fourteen years when lambs' wool yarn was used for the first time. By 1791 eight more frames had been added to the original four and sixty-five people were employed in their operation, 75 per cent of whom were women. Carding machinery had, during this period, been installed in Galashiels and this required the producers of Hawick to transport their wool by pony to be spun. The incentive was there then for carding and spinning machinery to be installed at Hawick and this was accomplished in 1804. Hawick was now firmly installed as the founder of the new industry in the Borders though other townships were not slow in following the lead. Hawick did, however, keep ahead in progress and expansion and by 1816 had 510 frames installed which produced 320,000 pairs of hose per annum: by 1844 there were 1,200 frames in the town and 2,605 in the area as a whole.

Tweed mill, Hawick.

All was not plain sailing and in the depression of the middle of the century "tramping money" was issued to help the people go to work in Leicester and Nottingham; this subsistence allowance amounted to 12s. 6d. (62½p) and was not much of an inducement to persuade the workers to move so far from their home area. Poor transport arrangements restricted the sale of the finished products to a very limited region and at times bad weather closed the roads and made trading impossible so that means of subsistence were still further attenuated. As late as a century ago wages amounted to no more than 18s. (90p) per week in return for very long working hours, though even this was better than the wages paid in areas further south in England.

22

The first power frame came to Hawick in 1858 and ten years later 90 were in use together with 800 hand frames. This resulted in a dramatic increase in production which, together with improved conditions on the roads and the coming of the railways, created a state of considerable prosperity by the end of the century.

In the days prior to the introduction of machine-operated frames the operatives sat on stools placing yarn over the needles while working a pair of levers with the hands and operating a series of treadles with the feet. Major inventions were made in the nineteenth century and these helped Hawick with its factory style production and division of labour while its competitors in other parts of the country continued to favour small scale manufacturing. At the turn of the century specialised knitwear, including cashmere, was being developed and markets opened in England through the usual wholesale and retail outlets, although very soon the middle man was eliminated and selling was done direct to retailers.

Trade unions were a new phenomenon with which the manufacturers had to contend but serious disputes have been rare. During both wars production was switched to clothing for the services but at least there was no shortage of raw materials, which meant an early return to normality once hostilities ceased, although the depression of the 1920's severely hit the industry. Since then, however, production has never looked back and the export market for the high quality goods is now world-wide.

The principal fibres used in knitwear are, of course, cashmere and wool. Cashmere is obtained from the Kashmir goat, indigenous to the mountainous areas of China, Kashmir and Tibet. The goat's coat is hand-plucked or, alternatively, the hair is collected where it has been shed naturally and as only the downy undercoat is used, amounting in weight to a mere few ounces per goat, it is understandable why cashmere garments are so expensive to produce and purchase. The wool used is sheared from the backs of living sheep in Australia and New Zealand, that obtainable from the local Cheviot sheep not being of the required quality. Both cashmere and wool are then passed through the processes of carding, dyeing and spinning to create suitable thread for use on the frames, which each weigh about four and a half tons and are capable of knitting between six and 12 garments of equal size at the same time.

As might be expected the manufacture of a garment from the prepared thread to its eventual marketing passes through several stages which will now be followed in general terms.

The first operation is the knitting of the ribbed bands for the cuffs and waists done appropriately enough on rib knitting machines which have two individual sets of needles controlled by a pattern drum which determines the type and size of rib required. A maximum of 24 parts can be knitted simultaneously and the bands come off the machine in a continuous roll, thus requiring cutting by hand into individual parts. The cut rib is next laid on a series of needles fixed to a bar with every rib stitch pierced by a needle. A tack row is provided to simplify the running on of the ribbed part on to the needles; a clean row of stitches is secured round the needles by leaving the knitted rows un-roved above the slack row.

The completed ribs are now transferred to the frame and the main part of the garment knitted to them. It is made in four separate parts—back, front and two sleeves—eight parts being knitted simultaneously at a rate of ninety rows per minute. The front and back are now joined across the shoulder line followed by the attachment of the sleeves. The front and back joining is achieved by a binding machine producing an "elastic" seam which allows the garment to stretch without breaking. A seaming machine deals with the sleeves and gives a strong but non-bulky seam able to withstand considerable stress.

The seaming is next reinforced by hand-sewing at the shoulder, armpits, waist-band and cuffs and at this point comes the first quality examination. While all this is going on the collars are manufactured on hand operated machines as are any trimmings that may be required. Each row is drawn by hand, the shape being formed by the manipulation of stitches to needles effected by hand controls. The collars and trimmings are then attached to the main body of the garment which is then scoured to remove oils applied during the processing of the yarn. This is done in a wooden tub rotating round a group of wooden beaters operating in soap flakes in softened water. If a pile is required to the garment this is done by the process of milling in a machine with wooden paddles. The garment is then rinsed in softened water, the temperature being gradually reduced as the process continues. A hydro-extractor next comes into operation to remove the water and leave the garment semi-dry. The drying process is completed by tumbler drying in which hot air is circulated through the garment, which is then decreased by having steam blown through while it is attached to a metal shape.

The first action of finishing the garment is the attachment of the collar, trimmings and buttons. As far as this stage there has been no opening for the head so the neck shape is now formed by hand cutting round a template after which a linking machine is used to secure the collar using an "elastic" stitch followed by the formation of buttonholes and the sewing on of the buttons, both of which operations are automated. Any finishing touches still required are done by hand sewing and the garment is once more examined for possible flaws. This is followed by steam pressing and the attachment of spare buttons and the ticket giving information on style, colour and size. The now complete garment is folded and placed in a polythene bag, the mouth of which is opened by a jet of air, and placed in a stockroom to await despatch.

Galashiels—church and mills.

Perhaps, on reflection, knitted ware is not so expensive after all considering that the hair or wool has to come from the far corners of the earth and there are so many operations to accomplish before the goods appear in the shops.

So far as industry is concerned it is natural to dwell on the manufacture of woollen wearing apparel for which the Borders area has for so long been

◀ Manderston House.

famous, but since the war a wide diversity of industrial output has been competing for the labour force. Electrical and mechanical engineering, precision tool making, printing, vegetable and fish freezing and processing, clothing and joinery manufacture, paper converting, photoprocessing and the manufacture of plastics and electronic and sports equipment are all carried out in some part or other of the region as well as the supporting construction industry and the more basic industries of agriculture, hill and sheep farming, inshore fishing and forestry. Add to all these the growing tourist trade with the necessity to provide transport, hotels, restaurants and such like and it is fair to assume that the future should be bright.

To accommodate this multiplicity of industrial expansion new factories, housing, schools and colleges are being built, including the new community of Tweedbank, situated between Galashiels, Melrose and Selkirk. This is an interesting development in that it is an industrial concept within a preserved country setting. The whole complex totals some 240 acres of which only 30 acres are devoted to industrialisation; of the remainder, 88 acres are occupied by housing and 122 acres given over to sport and recreation. The housing areas, with a planning density of 951 units, are in groups well screened from each other and from the industrial zone by extensive tree planting. The houses range in size from those having only one to those with up to four bedrooms to enable a well balanced community to develop, including those who are disabled; the industrial zone is given over to small developments ideally suited to the limited manpower available locally and which will in no way damage or destroy the environment.

The Borders region has neither the infrastructure nor the population to attract and support large industrial enterprises and is, therefore, not in a position even to attempt to induce large employers to move into the area. Small scale industry, preferably with a high turnover and reasonable profit margin is, however, ideally suited to the prevailing situation.

Agriculturally the Borders can conveniently be divided into three distinct zones, the lowlands ranging up to 400 feet, the uplands from 400-800 feet, and the hills above 800 feet.

The first classification comprises the land between Kelso and Berwick, roughly triangular in shape and known as the Merse, with a thick overlay of alluvium and glacial till interspersed with long, low drumlins* running east-west indicating the effect the Cheviots had on the geological ice flow. Its sheltered position, summer warmth and an average rainfall of less than 30 inches coupled with a soil cover of heavy clay loams render it a region of intensive cultivation, accomplished by extensive mechanisation. Approximately half the land is given over to grain crops, one-third to root crops such as potatoes, sugar-beet and swedes with the remainder devoted to grazing for farm-bred stock.

*Elongated hill or ridge formed by glacial pressure.

The rich agricultural land of the Merse.

The uplands is largely given over to stock farming, any arable production being used for fodder and not for cash as in the lowlands. The stock is mixed, comprising beef and dairy herds and sheep, the latter, as to be expected, being fatter and heavier than their counterparts on the hills and bred for meat rather than wool. Border Leicesters are crossed with Cheviots and the resulting progency crossed with Oxford Down. The farms of the uplands are generally smaller than those on the hills and occupy the area of the middle Tweed, Teviotdale and the lower slopes of the Cheviots and Lammermuirs, the flocks and herds feeding on grass pastures.

Above 800 feet the farms are of anything up to 6,000 acres in extent and occupy the high ground of Upper Tweeddale, the Cheviots, Lammermuirs and Moorfoots, being stocked with indigenous Linton Blackface sheep feeding on the heather pastures.

27

Generally speaking the Borders' weather is ideally situated to the production of cereals, particularly barley, and root, vegetable and soft fruit crops though the higher levels in the west and south are more often given over to grassland.

Drained podsolic* soils are characteristic of the Southern Uplands though parts are occupied by peat, the higher and less dry areas supporting a variety of moorland species — crowberry, heather, sphagnum and cotton and deer grasses. The spread of hill farming does seem to be gradually reducing these species, however, a gradual replacement taking place of various grass forms for grazing — bent, fescue, hair, mat and moor, which already occupy by far the greater part of the land not given over to forestry and which is too steep to support other than scrub birch, hazel, juniper and oak.

The low lying parts of the Southern Uplands are entirely controlled by man in some form or other and this has resulted in considerable and widespread changes in the natural soil and vegetation though many areas of marsh, woodland and hedgerow remain. Ploughing, fertilisation, planting, seeding, grazing and the general ramifications of intensive farming and horticulture have all had a profound and lasting effect on the landscape.

The buying and selling of stock from all three zones is centred on the largest auction market in southern Scotland at Newtown St Boswells while the Tweedmouth maltings assures a ready and handy disposal point for the principal grain crop, barley.

Beekeeping is an important sideline of the farmers and others who practice it as a profitable hobby. Honey production is carried on in all four counties, the heather of the high ground, the clover of the pastureland and the tree-clad valleys provide good foraging ground throughout the spring and summer.

Statistics issued by H.M.S.O. for 1974 show that the largest number of farms are in the middle acreage bracket:-

Size range	No.	Percentage
Up to 50 acres	165	11
50 to 125 acres	173	12
125 to 250 acres	212	15
250 to 500 acres	347	23
500 to 1,250 acres	396	27
1,250 to 2,500 acres	124	8
2,500 to 5,000 acres	49	3
Over 5,000 acres	12	1
	1478	100

*Any of a group of zonal soils that develop in a temperate to cold moist climate under coniferous or mixed forest or under heath vegetation and have an organic mat and thin organic mineral layer above a grey leached layer resting on an alluvial dark brown horizon.

Anyone passing through the Borders from the middle Tweed westwards cannot fail to be impressed by the huge areas covered by forests, some planted by private landowners but more often by the Forestry Commission which now has its headquarters in Edinburgh, an acknowledgement by Whitehall of Scotland's importance in this respect. The principal species is appropriately the Scots Pine, which is tolerant of dry conditions though a slow grower compared with other varieties. Some forests grow mixed timbers though principally conifers, including Norway and Sitka spruce and Lodgepole pine, ash, birch and oak are being produced in Yair Hill, Elibank and Traquair Forests. The success of these vast areas given over to timber production is due to the fact that there is very little land that is unplantable and the climate and terrain being ideal for tree growth. About 14 per cent of the land is forest covered, half is privately owned and half cultivated by the Forestry Commission.

A typical scene in the Tweed valley near Cardrona.

Apart from the growing and harvesting of the timber the Commission is actively engaged in the conservation and management of the wildlife that inhabits the forests, rivers and moors under its control. Timber production is naturally the prime purpose of the Commission's existence but in such an artifically created environment it is essential to maintain a correct balance between it and the various species to be found there. As distinct from foresters the Commission employs rangers, men with special knowledge of the countryside and its wildlife. Many harmless species such as badgers and otters are actively encouraged and all statutory laws that relate to animals, birds and plants are enforced. The rangers co-operate with local and national bodies and societies in the promotion and protection of rare species and often habitats are specially created with this end in view, though they are also provided for the more common species as well.

The forests are now becoming important recreational areas and the Commission is catering for this by providing forest walks and rides, exhibitions and observation hides. Fishing is encouraged and game shooting and deer stalking under proper supervision can be undertaken.

The rangers are also responsible for the annual deer culls which are necessary to keep down numbers to within feeding availability limits and to prevent excessive damage to young trees.

Perhaps the most surprising feature in any assessment of the industrial capacity of the Borders is the transport system, or rather lack of it. In contrast to many other parts of the British Isles there are no motorways and, since Dr Beeching wielded his axe, the only railway is the main east coast route passing through Berwickshire. There are only three trunk roads and they all run in a north-south direction. Many would incline to the view that railways, roads and airports play havoc with farming and tourist interests, destroying vast areas of agricultural land and discouraging the outsider to visit the area for recreational and holiday purposes. The opinion of others would be that if the railway system could be restored and a motorway or two laid down the prosperity of the Borders would be bound to improve. In the present economic climate it is unlikely that those who share the latter view will see their hopes realised in anything other than the very distant future, but in any case the area does not seem to be doing too badly even without the trappings and sophistication of modern transport arrangements.

CHAPTER FIVE

Leisure and Recreation

THE border area is a "natural" for all those who enjoy the open air and the freedom of wide-open spaces. Here one can participate in all the usual sports and recreations such as association and rugby football, bowls, camping and caravanning, cricket, curling and skating, fishing, golf, horse racing, motor racing and rallying, hunting, pony trekking—of which Daniel Defoe and his party may have been the earliest participants when they rode on horseback up Cheviot in 1728—riding, sailing, swimming, tennis and walking. Kelso is the centre for horse racing and Charterhall, a Second World War airfield between Coldstream and Lauder, for motor racing but the rest of the activities can be enjoyed virtually all over the region.

There is no gainsaying that the countryside is magnificent, and it is certainly one of the most beautiful and unspoilt areas of the British Isles with the rivers flowing through picturesque, well-wooded country, dotted with border keeps thick with memories of the stories into which they were woven by Sir Walter Scott; a contrasting land, not only of forest and sparkling rivers, but of hill, valley and quiet and secluded villages. No wonder George Borrow wrote "Which of the world's streams can Tweed envy with its beauty and renown". For nature lovers it is something of a paradise, in excess of nine hundred species of plants and two hundred and fifty of birds having been recorded in Berwickshire alone. Golden plover, grouse, merlin, peregrine falcon and partridge frequent the moors and at Hule Moss near Greenlaw thousands of pink-footed geese congregate in the autumn. The haunting and beautiful cries of the curlew and green plover are commonly heard, the latter being regarded as an unlucky bird in Covenanting times because the positions of those being pursued were frequently exposed by the birds' flight and "peewit" calls. Crossbills and siskins frequent the forested areas; frogs and toads are inhabitants of the more stagnant waters; the dipper prefers the faster flowing streams while the heron chooses the calmer waters where he can more easily see the fish and amphibians that make up his diet. Badger, blue hare, fox, otter, the ubiquitous rabbit, red squirrel, roe-deer, shrew, stoat, vole, weasel and the wild goat with its splendid horns and shaggy coat as well as lizards and snakes are widespread. While some species are not abundant all are there for those with patience to look, stand and stare. For the archeologically minded there is, as we have seen, plenty of evidence of ancient settlements, druid circles, iron age fortresses, burial mounds, standing stones, megaliths and Roman encampments.

The leisure activity most often associated with the Tweed and its tributaries is salmon and trout fishing which can be practised from Peebles right down to the preserve of the Salmon Fisheries Company at Berwick. The fishing rights are largely in private hands but visitors can obtain permits without too much difficulty from certain angling associations. Salmon fishing, and indeed perhaps all fishing, is something of an art and if it is to be prosecuted successfully requires considerable skill and patience and an aptitude for being able to cope with the prevailing weather conditions. Fishing

Quiet contemplation as the Tweed winds through Peeblesshire. *Scottish Tourist Board*

can be done from the bank, or a boat or by wading out into the water and can be carried out either by spinning with bait or with the aid of flies. Flies have been given rather fanciful names and are not flies at all but artificial lures known by such appellations as Torrish, Dusty Miller, Mar Lodge, Durham Ranger, Black Ranger, Jock Scott and the highly improbable Black Gold-finch: if it is trout that one is after then Blue Dunns, Silver and Greenwell's Glory, Teal, March Brown, Olives, Black and Grey Gnat, Smoke Fly, Orange Partridge, Knotted Midge, Poult and Waterhen Blow, Snipe and Purple, Needle Brown, Hackle Blue Upright and Dotterel are more the line. The choice of fly depends on several considerations such as wind strength, position of the sun, amount of light and shade, depth and state of the water and its temperature and the type of background to the point from where the line is cast. The salmon season is from the 1st February to 30th November, the early season fish being in the 6-12 lbs category gradually increasing in weight until by the autumn 18-25 lbs is usual. Brown trout can be taken from the 15th March to 6th October, daytime angling being best in April and May and evening fishing in the midsummer period. The usual catch weighs between one and two pounds but exceptionally four pounders are recorded.

Apart from the more well known salmon and trout angling, coarse fishing is widespread and dace, eel, pike, perch, roach and grayling are popular catches; indeed a recent survey of the Tweed river system contains no fewer than 16 different species of fish. For those who have caught their salmon or alternatively have been able to afford to buy a few pounds the following recipe for Tweed Kettle might come in useful: —

Ingredients: — 4 lbs middle cut salmon, fish stock, white wine, chopped chives or shallots and parsley, ground mace, 2-3 oz butter, salt and pepper.

Method: — Poach the salmon in the stock for about five minutes, remove skin and bones and cut into 2" pieces before returning to the stock to which should have been added the wine, seasoning and mace. Poach gently for ten minutes and then remove the fish and place in a serving dish. Next reduce the liquid by two thirds and add the chives or shallots and parsley and blend in the butter before pouring over the fish. Serve with peas and new potatoes.

This somewhat aristocratic delicacy is far removed from Rumbledethumps, another Borders dish of much less sophistication comprising boiled cabbage, potatoes, chives, onions and butter.

The resident and visitor alike have surely only themselves to blame if they cannot find some recreational pursuit to their liking. There can be few more enjoyable areas in which to unwind and relax but it is essentially for those whose basic leisure requirements are peace, quiet and solitude and who can appreciate beauty that seems, and almost certainly has, remained untouched for centuries.

CHAPTER SIX

Source to Peebles

FOR those entering Scotland from England as good a place as anywhere to cross the border is Gretna Green on the A74 from Carlisle. This village, the scene for so long of runaway marriages over the blacksmith's anvil and its signs of "Haste ye back to Scotland" aimed at those unfortunate enough to be travelling south, is a place best left to the curious eccentricities of our social behaviour. It is, however, on the road to our objective, the source of the Tweed. Proceeding north from Gretna the road passes through Ecclefechan with its associations of Thomas Carlyle, on past Lockerbie and over Beattock Summit on its way to Glasgow. To achieve our purpose it is at Beattock that the A74 has to be left and the A701 joined for Moffat, a golfing centre town of some 2,000 inhabitants picturesquely set amid hills extensively given over to sheep farming, an occupation finely symbolised by the statue of a ram standing on a rugged stone plinth in the High Street. The ubiquitous Robert Burns commemorated himself by scratching on a window of the *Black Bull* his famous verse about Mrs Davies: —

> "Why had she been formed so small and Mrs D. so big?"
> Ask why God made the gem so small
> And why so huge the granite
> Because God meant mankind should set
> That higher value on it."

The "trademark" of the upper Tweed valley —Ram Statue, Moffat.

The Devil's Beef Tub.

It is fine hill walking country, and a good angling area for those desirous of fishing the Annan and Moffat Water, but its popularity as a spa on account of a nearby sulphur spring has long since passed it by. A point of interest is that in the churchyard lies J. L. McAdam, the roadmaker, who gave his name to tarmacadam and who did so much in the last century to improve and extend travelling conditions throughout the country.

Five or six miles north of the town is an extraordinary declivity 500-600 feet deep known as the Devil's Beef Tub. It is a terminal valley deepened and widened by glacial action and has steep sides all round broken only by an outlet for the infant Annan. Its name is in all probability derived from the fact that it was a safe hideout for cattle and sheep thieves, known as "reivers", and their ill-gotten gains when rustling was a common place pastime in days when roads, if any, were mere tracks and the long arm of the law did not always extend far enough. South-west Scotland was the centre and springboard of the Covenanters and at the side of the road near the Beef Tub stands a memorial to one of them, John Hunter, who was shot "on the hillside opposite" in 1685. It was here that the worst excesses were perpetrated on both sides, excesses such as those committed by Graham of Claverhouse on the one hand and David Leslie at Philiphaugh on the other, about which more later. It was here also that churches were emptied and the people took to the hills to hold their services and take the sacrament in the heather under the wide open skies, guarded by posses of armed men on the look-out for the hated oppressors.

The Covenanters were, broadly speaking, supporters of the views of John Calvin and the Borders were a hotbed of his theology. He was born in Picardy in 1509 and was a famous theologian and reformer, who carried on the work of Martin Luther, spending most of his life in Basle and Geneva and dying in 1564. The practice of Calvinism is a theological system differentiating the Reformed from the Lutheran churches, emphasising the sovereignty of God and His "otherness" and is especially identified with the doctrine of pre-destination. Presbyterians, Independants, some sections of Baptists and nearly all French Protestants follow these tenets but their full implications are seldom accepted by Christian communities of the twentieth century. The position was, however, very different in the seventeenth century in the days of John Hunter and his like. They believed in the rejection of the episcopacy and that the organisation of the church was adequately served by elders and presbyters and, what is more, they were prepared to fight for their beliefs and against religious oppression.

Since the Reformation it had been Scotland's principle to oppose the Roman Catholic Church and covenants were drawn up and signed by those pledged to maintain Presbyterian doctrines as early as 1557 and again in 1581. Charles I and Archbishop Laud had the idea of implanting the English liturgy across the border and to this end it was decreed that the Book of Common Prayer should be read in every Scottish Church on Sunday, 23rd July, 1637. This provoked the famous action of the serving-maid, Jenny Geddes who, it might be said, struck the first blow for the Covenant when she hurled her stool at Dean Hannay in the pulpit of St Giles Cathedral, Edinburgh. This reading of the Book of Common Prayer was the spark that set off the religious fireworks which continued to explode for the next fifty years interspersed with conciliatory interludes, such as in 1643 when the Solemn League and Covenant was signed. Unfortunately this meant one thing to the Scots and another to the English, a religious principle to the former, a political one to the latter; Covenanters and Puritans found themselves on the same side but were fighting the royalists for different reasons, though there was a certain religious affinity. After Cromwell's success the Covenant was rejected in favour of Independancy and, after the Restoration, attempts by Charles II to impose episcopacy in Scotland were violently opposed, reaching a bitter and horrifying climax in 1679-80. It was not until 1688 that the struggle ended with the Glorious Revolution and from the following year Presbyterianism has maintained its hold as the Established Church of Scotland. It is worthy of note that Scotland passed from one extreme to the other: prior to the Reformation it was devoted to Roman Catholicism in a way that England never was but afterwards it displayed opposition to episcopacy and other trappings of Catholicism such as England never did.

Like all religious wars the fighting between the two sides to the dispute was conducted in such a ferocious manner that they were both guilty of the most monstrous atrocities. In contrast to the events of three centuries ago there takes place in the afternoon of the last Sunday of July in the quiet and peace of St Mary's Church of the Lowes in Yarrow what is known as a "blanking preaching". The service is held in the open to commemorate the fact that Covenanter preachers were not permitted to hold services inside churches and it is believed to have been held thus each year since Covenanting times.

A mile beyond the Beef Tub the road reaches the water-shed at a height of 1,334 feet and shortly after, at a distance of six miles from Moffat, passes the source of the Tweed at Tweed's Well. Travelling north, this is on the right of the road which now follows the left bank of the river until just before the junction with the road to Drumelzier.

Dr Pennecuick had this to say about the source — "From this fountain springeth Tweed, and runneth for the most part, with a soft yet trotting stream, towards the north-east, the whole length of the country (Peeblesshire), in several meanders." The area where the Tweed rises is also the source of the Annan and Clyde and though only half a mile apart at the start they soon go their separate ways, the Tweed to flow mainly in an easterly direction, the Annan almost due south and the Clyde to the north west. The Clyde just exceeds the Tweed in length, being 106 miles long, though the accolade of Scotland's longest river goes to the Tay which is 118 miles in length. The Tweedsmuir Hills where the three rivers rise are at the junction of Dumfries-shire, Lanarkshire and Peeblesshire and all gain strength from burns flowing from remote and attractive glens. One of the Tweed's tributaries, Biggar Water, rises in an area of marshland near Covington, with the Clyde flowing along the western boundary. This has a curious effect in times of excessive rainfall because then some Clyde water overflows into Biggar Water and thus ultimately finds its way into the Tweed.

This is an area little changed since the earth rose out of the sea and the ice-flows moulded the hills and valleys, an area wild and remote but beautiful and tranquil with little to break the silence except the calls of curlews, lapwings and skylarks. As might be expected it is also an area of reservoirs and until 1905 the infant Tweed was fed by Talla Water and Gameshope Burn but these were utilised to feed the Talla Reservoir which was constructed to supply the evergrowing demands for water of expanding Edinburgh. The water is carried by an aqueduct 22 miles long with 21 tunnels, the shortest of which is 133 yards long and the longest $1\frac{1}{3}$ miles under Wormal Hill opposite Stanhope valley. Five hundred and fifty men were employed on the project of whom about thirty were not destined to witness its completion; they lie buried in Tweedsmuir Churchyard. Below Tweedsmuir is the village of Drumelzier where Merlin the Magician is supposed to be buried. More authentic are the ruins of Tinnis Castle, blown up during the feud between two prominent border families, the Flemings and Tweedies. The Tweed initially flows northwards for 15 miles passing the hamlet of Tweedsmuir from which John Buchan took his title, and where in the old churchyard are headstones commemorating martyrs of Covenanting times. Among them is that of John Hunter, inscribed: —

> "Here lyes John Hunter martyr who was cruelly murdered at Corehead by Col. James Douglas and his party for his adherance to the word of God and Scotland's Covenanted Work of Reformation 1685."

Storm clouds over the source of the River at Tweed's Well; reafforestation on the hills.
Forestry Commission

The river then turns eastwards towards Peebles and once this change of direction has occurred it is barely deviated from in the remainder of its long journey to the sea at Berwick-upon-Tweed, during which it drains a watershed of 1,850 square miles.

Peeblesshire is probably the most attractive inland county of the Southern Uplands. The county town up to local government re-organisation in 1974 was Peebles, the name of which is derived from "pebyll" meaning a hut, tent or habitation. A royal burgh since the fourteenth century and sharing with the Shire the probability of being the most popular inland health and holiday resort of southern Scotland, it is attractively situated astride the river and screened on all sides by hills.

The old town stands on Eddleston Water to the west of its new counterpart and was granted its royal charter in 1367 by Robert Bruce's son, David II. St Mungo, the founder of Glasgow, is reputed to have visited the town in the sixth century and a well named after him supposedly commemorates the visit. David I (1124-53) built the castle and it became a favourite residence of succeeding monarchs, possibly because of the good hunting in the neighbouring hills which form the northern part of the Ettrick Forest. There is an interesting thirteenth century Cross Kirk and the town has links with Mungo Park, John Buchan and William and Robert Chambers who were Walter Scott's publishers. Mungo Park's surgery was on the south side of the High Street in what is now the *Keg Bar and Restaurant* and his house is in Northgate; John Buchan once resided in the last house at the west end of the High Street.

Like other Border towns Peebles holds an annual festival, the Beltane Festival, in June, which has its origins in the old Celtic custom of the lighting of bonfires on the summits of hills on May Day, Beltane meaning "fire". The celebration originally marked the beginning of summer and the victory of light over darkness; the coming of winter and the commencement of darkness being marked on the 1st November by Samhain. This festival marked the end of harvest and the onset of the short days and long nights of the most arduous season of the year. The fires that were to burn until springtime were kindled, the future was foretold by the casting of spells and burnt offerings were made to propitiate the gods. It was believed that the spirits of the dead roamed the earth doing evil and firebrands were carried round the settlements to ward them off. Also surplus livestock, for which there would be little or no food during the long winter months, were slaughtered and the meat salted and stored.

We have barely started our journey down river before encountering the salmon which is so much associated with the Tweed and its tributaries. This first meeting is the depiction of three fishes on the town's coat of arms; one of the salmon is shown swimming downstream and the others upstream and the

Latin motto of "contra nando incrementum" translated means "there is increase by swimming against the tide" or perhaps "success will come by resisting obstacles".

The *Cross Keys Inn* dates from 1653 and figures in Sir Walter Scott's novel, *St Ronan's Well,* for it was its first landlady, Marion Ritchie, who became Scott's heroine, Meg Dodds, with the hotel transformed into the *Cleikum Inn.* Marion is reputed to haunt the room which was her bedroom and various phenomena which have occurred from time to time are supposedly due to the machinations of her ghost. These vary from a guest sleeping in the room waking up in the hall, to beer taps being turned off, to a vacuum cleaner floating through the air, to a member of the staff being pushed downstairs and breaking his ankle. As recently as September 1975 Marion was at work upsetting none other than the B.B.C., whose interviewer was attempting to make a recording about the apparition. Everything showed the operation to have been satisfactory but when the tape was played back it was blank. This was repeated twice more and then at the fourth attempt it worked but unfortunately at twice the normal speed and this despite a fail safe lock on the recording instrument which should have prevented any accidental speed change.

There are two notable gardens in the vicinity of Peebles. Between the town and the village of Bellspool eight miles up river are Dawyck House Gardens noted for woodlands with rare trees and shrubs, narcissus and rhododendrons. The first horse chestnuts in Scotland were planted in 1650 and the first larches in 1725. The estate has been in existence for over three hundred years and during this time has been owned by three families, the Veitches, Naismyths and Balfours. It has one of the finest collections of specimen trees in the land and the arboretum, which is open to the public, has recently been presented to the nation by Lt. Col. A. N. Balfour and is now an out-station of the Royal Botanic Gardens. There is a noted heronry in the Lour Wood and Japanese Sika deer can be seen on the surrounding hills.

Two and a half miles south east of the town are Kailzie Gardens with a fine variety of flowers, plants and trees, walled and wild gardens, a wildfowl park and greenhouses to delight the connoisseur. Close by is ruined Horsburgh Castle.

Just upstream from Peebles, Manor Water joins the Tweed from the south and is crossed by a bridge which is on the Wemyss and March estate. It was built in 1702 by the Earl of March to a design of his father, William, Duke of Queensberry. Close by the Tweed is also crossed by a bridge, both structures crossing the waters where there were formerly fords.

The road up Manor Water reaches a dead end before the head of the stream is reached but the main interests of the valley are in its lower reaches.

Threatening sky over Peebles.

Here it was that David Ritchie built himself a cottage which was later rebuilt for him, to somewhat better standards, by the local laird, Sir James Naismyth of Passo. This habitation was known as the Black Dwarf's cottage because David was only three and a half feet tall and known locally as Bowed Davie o' the Wuddus. Regrettably his neighbours made fun of him and consequently he did not get on very well with them, except for the children with whom he seems to have had a special affinity; he was also well known for his love of wild creatures and is commemorated by a stone figure in the valley.

David believed he had mystical powers and his mental and physical qualities made him of interest to the local medical fraternity, including Dr Mungo Park who was then practising in Peebles. When David died he was buried in Kirkton Manor Churchyard but about ten years later his remains were disinterred and taken to Glasgow Hospital for study purposes. This was in spite of the warning inscribed on the headstone of his grave: —

"Good friend! for Jesus' sake forbear
To dig up dust enclosed here;
Blest be the man that spares these stones,
And curst be he that moves my bones."

Sir Walter Scott visited David at his cottage and subsequently wrote *The Black Dwarf* based on his life story. At the time of Scott's visit in 1797 the author was staying at "Hallyards" in the hamlet of Glack with Dr Adam Ferguson, who was Professor of Moral Philosophy at Edinburgh University; it was at the doctor's house in the capital that the famous meeting between Robert Burns and Scott took place.

Glack, meaning a hollow between two hills, is reached by deviating off the Manorhead road onto a side road leading back towards the Tweed but terminating also in a dead-end, at which is Barns House, a Georgian mansion built between 1773 and 1780 by James Burnet. The surrounding land was acquired in the fifteenth century by James' ancestors, one of whom, the fourth laird, was known as "The Hoolet", a name acquired because of his owl-like night vision which he was reputed to put to good use during raids on his neighbours' cattle and sheep. He died at the age of one hundred and seven, leaving behind him the old tower of Barns which now lies in ruins near the mansion and was used by John Buchan as the setting for *John Burnet of Barns*.

John Buchan was born in Peebles on the 26th August 1875, son of the Rev. John Buchan and his wife Helen, and spent many holidays at his maternal grandfather's farmhouse at Broughton between Biggar and Peebles. John wrote in 1901 — "Since ever I was a very little boy I have liked Broughton better than any other place in the world." This despite the tragic memory he must have retained all his life of the death of his five year old sister, Violet. She is buried in the local churchyard with other members of the Masterton family.

Eventually John moved from the Borders to live in the Oxfordshire village of Elsfield and there his remains are buried, but in his own words—"The Border hills were my own possession, countryside in which my roots went deep".

Close to Kirkton Manor on the east bank of Manor Water is Hundleshope House which was occupied for some two hundred years, before they moved to Lanarkshire, by ancestors of William Ewart Gladstone, the Victorial Liberal Prime Minister. The house was later occupied by a leading Jacobite, David Scott, who was friendly with John Murray, Bonnie Prince Charlie's secretary who lived at Broughton. Murray arranged with Scott for all the incriminating evidence in his house—diaries, cyphers, papers and letters—to be removed for safe-keeping by Scott who was sufficiently unwise to bury them in the garden of Hallmanor House on the river's west bank opposite Hundleshope. Unfortunately for Scott his erstwhile friend was captured and, in hope of saving himself from execution, turned informer; ever after he was referred to as "Mr Evidence Murray". Murray's house, Broughton Place, is a model defence tower, white harled, tall and splendid and situated in the rolling countryside of the upper Tweed valley. At one time it was the home of Baroness Elliot of Harwood, widow of Sir Walter who had a distinguished political career and served in Chamberlain's government as Secretary of State for Scotland and in Churchill's administration as Minister of Health.

The valley of Manor Water has several remains of ancient buildings, one of which is known as Macbeth's Castle, though it has no connection with Shakespeare's villain. The name is a corruption of Malbeth, a twelfth century High Sheriff of Tweeddale. Opposite the castle are the ruins of an early sixteenth century peel tower close by the House of Passo. Near the head of Glenrath Burn are traces of an ancient settlement excavated in 1939 and described in a 1967 publication—"Inventory of the Ancient Monuments of Peeblesshire". Near these sites is a third one, that of St Gordian's Chapel, almost certainly misnamed, since excavations carried out in 1935 revealed the traces to be, what is considered, those of a sixteenth century peel tower; this in spite of the unearthing of a stone with sixth century Christian markings which is now in Peebles Museum. It is thought that the Chapel once stood on the site now occupied by Kirkton Manor Church. At Castlehill are the ruins of yet another peel tower built by the Lowes family in the fifteenth century.

At one time the valley was famous for the quality and hunting ability of its birds of prey and many Scottish kings and members of the nobility had the local eyries raided and the captured birds trained to falconry.

Fame of a different character attended the valley in the last century when it was frequented by Burke and Hare, the notorious body snatchers. Both men were itinerant workers on the roads and they also sold fish from a cart in the surrounding villages, using the same cart on their return journeys to Edinburgh to transport the exhumed bodies for dissection by the capital's medical profession. Eventually fate caught up with them and Burke was executed in Edinburgh due, in part at least, to the fact that Hare turned King's evidence. Hare was later smuggled out of Scotland to the United States: this did him very little good because he was recognised and the angry citizens threw him into a lime kiln where he was blinded and severely burned. He returned to England and took to begging in London's Oxford Street in the 1850s.

Corresponding to Manor Water flowing to the Tweed from the south is Lyne Water joining from the north, distinguished by the ruins of Drochil Castle near Romannobridge; the castle was left unfinished in 1581 because its owner, Regent Morton, had been executed, ostensibly for complicity in Darnley's murder.

Neidpath Castle, high on the banks of the Tweed above Peebles. *Scottish Tourist Board*

Bordering the Tweed there are many fine abbey and castle ruins full of interest to the visitor and the first of these is Neidpath Castle, a Fraser stronghold, magnificently situated on a rocky crag above the river where it winds through a narrow gorge one mile upstream from Peebles. It dates from the early fourteenth century though substantial alterations were made in the seventeenth century. From it fine views of the river and its surroundings can be obtained and, because of its situation and the fact that it has walls eleven feet thick, it is understandable why the occupants held out longer than those in any other fortress in southern Scotland against the depredations of Cromwell's artillery in 1650.

The castle once belonged to Simon Fraser of Lovat whose head eventually ended up next to that of Wallace on London Bridge. His daughter married Gilbert de Haya of Yester whose family originally came from Normandy and which probably derived its name from the high hedges of the Cotentin Peninsula, known locally as "haies". The Hays remained lairds until the end of the seventeenth century, when the Duke of Queensberry purchased the castle from the first Marquis of Tweeddale. When the unmarried fourth Duke died in 1810 the dukedom devolved on the Scotts of Buccleuch and the castle passed to the Earl of Wemyss and March. The Marquis of Tweeddale was responsible for the erection of the Renaissance style arched gateway decorated with strawberries, a small bunch of which hang below the keystone under a goat's head, forming the Hay family crest.

Neidpath was the setting of a story which so impressed Sir Walter Scott that he immortalised it in verse: —

"He came — he passed — a heedless gaze,
As o'er some stranger glancing,
Her welcome spoke in faltering phrase,
Lost in his courser's prancing —
The Castle arch, whose hollow tone,
Returns each whisper spoken,
Could scarcely catch the feeble moan,
Which told her heart was broken."

The affair concerned the affection of a son of the Laird of Tushielaw for the daughter of an Earl of March although, unhappily, the girl's parents disapproved of the proposed marriage. The young man decided it would be best for both of them if he went abroad so that they could each try to forget and start a new life. Upon his departure the girl became very ill and her father eventually realised that only by reuniting the couple could his daughter's life be saved. Sadly the illness had so affected her appearance that when the laird's son returned he rode past the house without recognising her though she was waiting for him on the balcony and so she died, as Scott said, of a broken heart.

CHAPTER SEVEN

Peebles to Selkirk

THE towns of Innerleithen and Walkerburn are noted tweed-milling communities about a third of the way along the eighteen mile stretch of road which closely follows the river between Peebles and Selkirk. Innerleithen, where Leithen Water joins the Tweed, was turned into a thriving burgh from a hamlet by a blacksmith from nearby Traquair. Alexander Brodie went in 1751 to London where he made a fortune, in spite of living in Carey Street, before returning home to start the first woollen mill in the town.

In 1788 the worthy Alexander caused a "factory to be erected to give employment to the people of his native district, and for the object of promoting a spirit of industry among them". Production started in 1790 and in due course the factory became one of the largest and best equipped in the Borders. When it is considered that Alexander left home with just 17s. 6d. (87½p) in his pocket his is a remarkable story of achievement and philanthropy for which Innerleithen and Walkerburn have much to be thankful. No wonder Thomas Telford considered him "first in his profession and a man of the greatest ingenuity and integrity".

Innerleithen from the south bank of the Tweed.

Leithen Water, from which the town takes its name, is a beautiful little tributary and is remarkable that although only twelve miles in length it falls 1,200 feet between its source and junction with the Tweed, picking up on its way waters from the streams of Craighope, Woolandlee, Glentress and Blakenhopebyres. Short though it is it provides anglers, naturalists and country lovers in general with much to enjoy.

Scott's novel, *St Ronan's Well*, was the catalyst that made Innerleithen a fashionable watering place and it is recorded that in 1827 when its population amounted to no more than 447 souls it accommodated 1,438 people who had gone there to partake of the waters. The springs had been known before the end of the eighteenth century for their medicinal properties and were at that time known as Doo's Well but the name was changed to that of the novel soon after it was published and this name is perpetuated in the games held annually in July.

Opposite Innerleithen stands Traquair House where Quair Water runs into the Tweed. The name Traquair is derived from "Tra" meaning a dwelling or a hamlet and "Quair" meaning a stream with a wandering course. Originally the house was known as Traquair Castle and was granted a charter by Alexander I in 1107, he being the first of a long line of English and Scottish monarchs, twenty-seven in all, to have stayed there. It remained a royal demesne until the thirteenth century and was a popular resort of the nobility to exercise their enjoyment of hawking, fishing and hunting bear, boar and wolf. This Stuart (now Maxwell Stuart) family mansion dating from the tenth century is the oldest inhabited house in Scotland. Between 1633 and 1861 it was the seat of the Earls of Traquair, the first holder of the title being Charles I's Lord High Treasurer of Scotland.

By the late thirteenth century the house had become established as one of the network of fortified towers spread out along the Tweed valley to give warning of and guard against the frequent incursions of the English on their marauding raids from the south. Traquair and Neidpath are the best of these remaining defensive dwellings which eventually formed a chain along which smoke signals could be passed from one to the other in times of danger. The present whitewashed mansion grew out of this Border tower and is very picturesque.

At one time salmon fishing could take place from some of the windows so closely did the river flow to the walls. However, convenient though this might have been, greater was the inconvenience caused by periodic flooding and one of the Traquair dynasty had the course diverted to prevent such undesirable occurrences. On each side of one of the gateways is a carved bear on a stone plinth, mentioned by Scott in *Waverley* as the Bears of Bradendine. There is some reason to suppose that the gates may in fact be a folly since old prints show the area around them as grazing land with no carriageway.

Another version is that they were closed by the seventh Earl on the death of his wife in 1796 and that he vowed they would not be opened again until another countess resided in the house. This has never happened, since on the death of the bachelor eighth Earl in 1861 the title became extinct.

Yet a third theory relates to the seventh Earl who, according to Scott, closed the gates after entertaining Bonnie Prince Charlie who had left his army at Kelso in 1745 to try to persuade the Earl to rise in his support. On the Prince's departure the Earl pledged that the gates would be not be re-opened until a Stuart monarch was again crowned in London. The gates were erected in 1737-8 and stand in splendid isolation at the head of a tree-lined grassed avenue directly in front of the house, the actual driveway being many yards away to the right.

The treasures of the house include books, embroidery, glass, manuscripts and pictures, including Mary Queen of Scots' crucifix, rosary and purse and a silk quilt which she worked with her ladies-in-waiting, known as the "Four Maries". There are also letters written by Mary and the King's Room contains the bed in which she slept at Terregles House, near Dumfries. It was there in May, 1568, that she decided to seek the mercy in England of her cousin, Elizabeth, contrary to the advice of Lord Herries, her friend and host. Terregles is now demolished but many of its treasures can be found at Traquair.

Sir Walter Scott's "Bears of Bradendine"; the famous Bear Gate at Traquair House.

Apart from the mementos of Mary in the house, Traquair has another interesting connection with the Queen in that, at the time of her marriage to Darnley, she knighted John Stuart and appointed him Captain of the Guard, a position he retained on the succession of James VI. John was not only a trusted adviser of the Queen but a friend in need as it was he who organised her night escape from Holyrood House in Edinburgh and flight to Dunbar after the conspiracy and subsequent murder in 1565 of her favourite, David Rizzio. A year later John had the honour of entertaining Mary and Darnley when they stayed at Traquair for the hunting, and the cradle of their baby son, James VI, is a prized possession of the house. It might be thought that this close relationship with Mary was responsible for, or because of, the family's adherence to Catholicism, but this came later during the reign of Charles I. On a state visit to Scotland the King granted an Earldom to the then John Stuart and it was his heir, also named John, who married a daughter of the Marquis of Huntley and, on her death a year later, took for his second wife her sister-in-law, Lady Anne Seton. It was Anne who implanted the firm foundations of the Catholic religion, masses being frequently celebrated in a room at the top of the house, chosen for the fact that it had an escape exit for officiating priests down a staircase hidden at the back of a cupboard. The room also commanded a good view of the surroundings and this and the staircase went some way to ensuring the safety of both family and priests when the house was searched, as it was at intervals, for signs of popery. The present chapel dates from the mid-nineteenth century when Catholic emancipation was introduced to Scotland and the family became free to worship openly.

One of the most famous escapes from the Tower of London has Traquair connections for it was from the house that Lady Nithsdale set out to organise her husband's escape on the eve of his proposed execution. The fourth Earl of Traquair and his bride, daughter of the fourteenth Earl of Nithsdale had the political and religious convictions of the Jacobites and Traquair became a centre of the cause in the Borders. The redoubtable and brave Lady Nithsdale was the Countess of Traquair's sister-in-law and there is little doubt that plans of the escape plot were prepared by the secluded banks of Quair Water and subsequently successfully accomplished.

The grounds have standing in them several old bothies converted into craft workshops. In these the visitor can watch silk screen printing, weaving and woodworking being undertaken as well as pottery and the making of jewellery. Then after a stroll along the woodland walk on the banks of the Quair and Tweed, if refreshment is called for, a visit to the two hundred-year-old brewhouse to partake of home-brewed Traquair ale will in all probability prove a tempting diversion. Those who prefer something of a milder nature can partake of refreshments in the cottage tearoom which dates from 1745.

The Earl of Buchan, uncle of James III, acquired Traquair and bestowed it on his son, James Stuart, who became its laird and from whom the present family is descended. The property was purchased for £3. 15s. 10d. (£3.79p) from William Rogers, one of James III's favourites who had received it as a gift from the king. In 1492 a group of nobles, including Buchan, hanged the unfortunate Rogers from Lauder Bridge with five other favourites, who like him, had become unpopular at court.

Another fine estate is situated a mile or so upstream from Innerleithen. The beautiful mansions of Glenormiston stands in an estate of 900 acres and was bought for £25,500 in 1849 by Dr William Chambers, who was one of Peebles' most distinguished citizens and at the time head of the famous Edinburgh publishing firm of W. & R. Chambers. In 1883 it was sold to the Thorburn family, one of whose members had the honour of presenting the estate redendo, namely one red rose, to King George V and Queen Mary when they visited the house in July, 1923.

Walkerburn, just downstream from Innerleithen, similarly takes its name from the tributary which here joins the parent stream. The town, like its twin, owes its economic prosperity to the foresight and business acumen of one man, Henry Ballantyne, a textile manufacturer whose name is still synonymous with the firm he founded and which is still one of the main employers of the area. The Scottish Museum of Wool Textiles clearly depicts the expansion of the Scottish textile trade and has much of interest, including spinning demonstrations.

After traversing Peeblesshire for about 35 miles the river crosses into Selkirkshire a mile below Walkerburn by way of a narrow break at Elibank. Hereabouts, under the shadow of the 1,856 feet high Minchmore is Cheesewell, so called from the habit of travellers dropping into its waters cheese crumbs in order to propitiate the fairies reputed to haunt the spot.

Selkirk stands on Ettrick Water and is an ancient and notable royal burgh dating from 1535 and is noted for the manufacture and dyeing of tweed as well as being a market town. It has many connections with Walter Scott, who was at one time sheriff of the county and to whose memory a statue has been erected in the market square. Many relics of the great man are preserved in the court house and town hall, including his bench and chair. The *County Hotel* dates from the early nineteenth century and is a good example of the traditional coaching inn which has in its time accommodated Robert Southey, James Hogg, John Wesley and the Duke of Wellington, as well as being frequented by Walter Scott when he attended meetings of the Forest Club. Another connection with a famous man is provided by the ruins of the Auld Kirk in the aisle of which lie members of the Murray family, maternal ancestors of Franklin Delano Roosevelt, President of the United States of America during the Second World War.

The imposing and symbolic statue of Mungo Park in Selkirk's High Street.

In High Street there is a monument to Mungo Park, born in a cottage at nearby Foulshiels in 1771 and who was destined to meet his death far away on the Niger. Mungo died at Boussa in 1806 and over twenty years later in 1827 his son Thomas died at Aovamboo while trying to obtain information about his famous father. The monument also commemorates Thomas and another member of the expedition, Alexander Anderson, who died at Sansanding on the 22nd October 1805. Other memorials include those to Tom Scott, the artist and J. B. Selkirk the poet, whose real name was John Buchan Brown, but perhaps the most impressive is the one by Thomas Clapperton commemorating the scores that died at Flodden. It was erected in 1913, the 400th anniversary of the battle. Appropriately the statue is of a man-at-arms on foot, with halberd and standard with the simple inscription "O Flodden Field". A further connection with the battle is preserved in the museum; this relic is the flag brought back to the town from the battlefield by a man named Fletcher who was the sole survivor of Selkirk's 80 volunteers. The incident is annually commemorated during the common riding celebrations when the burgh standard-bearer "casts the colours" in the market place just as Fletcher threw down the flag intimating he was the sole survivor. There cannot be many towns that can boast of an ironmongery museum but Selkirk has one that contains a fine collection of old iron. The town is also one of few to give its name to a table delicacy—a largish, round flat cake, stuffed with raisins and peel, spiced and sugared and known as a Selkirk bannock. The well-known apellation "Souter", originally meaning "shoemaker", is reserved solely for those born in the town and cannot be acquired by outsiders no matter how long they might have resided in the burgh.

A Souter is the central character of a famous local ghost story which concerns one Rabbie Heckspeckle who was the town's best known busybody and nosey parker. One day a stranger called at his shop and while taking measurements for the pair of shoes he ordered Rabbie endeavoured to find out by elaborate questioning who the customer might be and from whence he came, but all to no avail. The stranger left saying he would return next day for his order and in the meantime Rabbie tried to establish the customer's identity by quizzing other customers who called at the shop. He was somewhat disconcerted to find that the stranger apparently resembled a man who had lived some distance out of Selkirk and had died recently. As promised the stranger called for his shoes the next day and was followed out of the shop by the inquisitive Rabbie. The trail led to the churchyard where the stranger lay down by a tombstone and vanished. The terrified shoemaker dashed back to town with his astonishing story and it was decided to open the grave; when this was done, the corpse within was found to be wearing a new pair of shoes! The body was re-interred in a new coffin but not before Rabbie had recovered the shoes, reasoning that after all they were not much use to a corpse, and placed them on sale in his shop. Alas for poor Rabbie; soon afterwards he disappeared and on the grave being re-opened it was found that the corpse was not only wearing the shoes but Rabbie's nightcap as well.

Four miles south west of Selkirk is the Duke of Buccleuch and Queensberry's seat at Bowhill-in-Yarrow. The fine Georgian house stands amid splendid scenery, was formerly the Border home of the Scotts of Buccleuch and is the ancestral home of Alice, Duchess of Gloucester, third daughter of the seventh Duke of Buccleuch and ninth Duke of Queensberry, who before her marriage was Lady Alice Cristobel Montague Douglas Scott.

Bowhill has relics of Monmouth, Queen Victoria and Scott, including Monmouth's cradle, saddlery and harness, cap, handkerchief, teething coral and the shirt he wore at his execution; the Queen's fan and several letters written in her own handwriting and Scott's plaid and the manuscript of "The Lay of the Last Minstrel" which includes the famous lines referring to this beautiful place:-

"When summer smiled on sweet Bowhill,
Any July's eve, with balmy breath,
Waved the blue-bells on Newark-heath;
When throstles sung in Hare-head shaw,
And corn was green on Carterhaugh,

And flourished, broad, Blackandro's oak,
The aged Harper's soul awoke!"

The many beautiful rooms contain fine examples of antique clocks, porcelain, silver and Mantegna designed tapestries as well as French furniture with Aubusson needlework. Works of art, miniatures and paintings abound and the latter include works by Canaletto, Claude, Gainsborough, Guardis, Hilliard, Holbein, Leonardo da Vinci, Raeburn, Reynolds, Ruysdael and Wilkie. The restored nineteenth century kitchen with its spit and brightly polished copper utensils is at the same time a modern housewife's delight or nightmare.

The surrounding area was once part of the Caledonian Forest, thickly covered with birch, hazel, oak and pine and abounding with boar, deer and wild cattle. It was a royal demesne forest under the nominal control of the Black Douglas' but they were eventually subdued by the Crown and the Red Douglas' and out of the ensuing shambles the Scotts of Buccleuch were able to assert themselves. The forest caused a considerable amount of trouble to succeeding monarchs since it was a secure hideaway for freebooters and other fugitives from justice but it was not until the reign of James V that a policy of deforestation was seriously pursued in an endeavour to destroy the areas of refuge for malefactors. It is here in the old forest that Ettrick and Yarrow meet two miles west of Selkirk and flow as Ettrick to join the Tweed five miles further on at Abbotsford.

"Sweet Bowhill"; the Duke of Buccleuch and Queensberry's Georgian mansion at Bowhill-in-Yarrow.

Yarrow Water and the countryside through which it flows are delightful indeed, a region of burn, loch, moor and mountain. Some are inclined to think of the beauty as being of a melancholy nature whilst others find it exhilarating, probably being unaware of the associated history and legend and perhaps having come upon it on a bright sunny day.

Half-way between Bowhill and Selkirk is the village of Philiphaugh, peaceful enough nowadays but the scene of terrible carnage in 1645 when the Royalist army under the command of James Graham, Earl of Montrose, was defeated by the Covenant forces commanded by General David Leslie. This disaster to Charles I's troops ensured the defeat of his cause in Scotland and the end of his episcopalian hopes for the country. Leslie was rewarded with a sum of 50,000 marks (about £33,000), a gold chain and ennoblement as Lord Newark. He was half-brother of the Marquis of Salisbury, grandson of Robert Stewart, Earl of Orkney, and a great-grandson of James V, but this illustrious ancestry did nothing to raise his standards above the level of a barbarian after his victory. The battle was an unequal-sided affair from the start since Montrose's force, only six hundred strong, was faced by opponents ten times his in strength. Add to this the fact that the Earl of Traquair had betrayed Montrose by informing Leslie of the disposition and weaknesses of his little company and it was obvious that, barring a miracle, there could be only one outcome of the battle even before hostilities commenced. A miracle did not occur and the six hundred were routed and destroyed. All who were captured, including some two hundred grooms, cooks and other non-combatants, together with three hundred women and children, were ruthlessly murdered in the name of religion. Over a hundred of the prisoners were shot in the courtyard of nearby Newark castle which stands on a mound above the rushing Yarrow a mile west of Bowhill and which was visited by Scott and Wordsworth. The castle was built about 1423 by Archibald, Earl of Douglas and was the home of Anna Scott, Countess of Buccleuch, the widow of Charles II's son by Lucy Walters, the ill-fated Duke of Monmouth who was created Duke of Buccleuch and Earl of Dalkeith on his marriage and who was executed after Sedgemoor for claiming the throne. A handful of Royalists, including Montrose, escaped from the castle and were refused sanctuary at Traquair House by the first Earl.

The cottage where Mungo Park was born stood opposite the castle and it was there that, after returning home in 1797, he wrote part of the story of his travels in West Africa. He was apprenticed at the age of fifteen to Dr Thomas Anderson who was then living in what are now Selkirk's Municipal Buildings. Later he served as a ship's doctor in the East Indies before agreeing to endeavour to discover the source of the Niger under the auspices of the African Association. To this end he led two expeditions; during the first from 1795-97 he reached the river from Senegal after many hardships and traced a small part of its course. He was one of 38 Europeans in the second expedition which set out in 1805 and from which not one returned. Fortunately he had the foresight to send back his journal to Gambia when the dangers of the journey became acute and it was subsequently published.

The splendour of St Mary's Loch.

The A708 follows the course of the Yarrow westwards passing Yarrow Church, about three hundred and forty years old, and where Scott's great-grandfather was minister, to St Mary's Loch and *Tibbie Shiels Inn* and eventually the road wends its way after 34 miles to Moffat, the starting point of our journey. However, our stopping point is the area of the Loch and its famous inn, a place of great grandeur and wild and splendid scenery, which Scott featured in "Marmion". The loch, situated amongst green hills, is four miles long with the delightful but smaller Loch o' the Lowes at its head. In the far distant past these two lochs were one but became separated by glacial deposits from the Crossleuch and Oxeleuch Burns.

55

Statue of James Hogg, the "Ettrick Shepherd", overlooking *Tibbie Shiels Inn*, St Mary's Loch and the Loch o' the Lowes.

Tibbie Shiels Inn.

On this narrow spit of land stands the *Tibbie Shiels Inn*, which has its unusual name from the maiden name of Mrs Richardson who died at the age of ninety-four and was one of its hostesses. The inn was a popular meeting place for Thomas Carlyle, Thomas de Quincey, Walter Scott, Robert Louis Stevenson and the "Ettrick Shepherd", James Hogg, who died in 1835 and is commemorated by a statue at the south end of St Mary's Loch. He stands there wistfully contemplating *Tibbies,* the scene of some of his most vivid earthly pleasure, while his dog looks down the valley towards their home on Altrive Lake where Hogg settled in 1817 on land owned by the Duke of Buccleuch. Hogg had a great affection for his sheep-dog and expressed his thoughts in perhaps the most beautiful and poignant poem ever written about man's best friend: —

"Come, my auld, towzy, trusty friend,
What gars ye look sae dung wi' wae?
D'ye think my favour's at an end,
Because thy head is turning grey?

Although thy strength begins to fail,
Its best was spent in serving me;
An' can I grudge thy wee bit meal,
Some comfort in thy age to gie?

O'er past imprudence, oft alane,
I've shed the saut and silent tear;
Then, sharin' a' my grief and pain,
My puir auld friend came snoovin' near.

For a' the days we've sojourned here,
And they've been neither fine nor few,
That thought possesst thee year to year
That a' my griefs arose frae you.

Wi' waesome face and hingin' head,
Thou wadst hae pressed thee to my knee
While I thy looks as well could read,
As thou hadst said in words to me:

'Oh, my dear master, dinna greet;
What hae I ever done to vex thee?
See, here I'm cowerin' at thy feet,
Just take my life, if I perplex thee.

Whatever wayward course ye steer;
Whatever sad mischance oe'rtake ye;
Man, here is ane will hold ye dear!
Man, here is ane will ne'er forsake ye.

When my last bannocks on the hearth,
Of that thou sanna want they share;
While I hae house or hauld on earth,
My Hector shall hae shelter there.

And should grim death thy noddle save,
Till he has made an end o' me;
Ye'll like a wee while on the grave
O ane wha aye was kind to thee."

He was a romantic poet of some repute and his work was highly thought of by both his friends, Carlyle and Scott. Scott in particular gave considerable practical help to the "Ettrick Shepherd", his self-chosen title, and introduced him to publishers and Edinburgh society. Hogg, however, was something of a rough diamond and was never able to adapt himself to the idiosyncracies of polite society, probably because he did not try very hard and also had the misfortune to be the possessor of a bad temper, characteristics which were not conducive to acceptance into the salons of the capital. He came from a line of foresters and shepherds which had a long tradition of feyness and witchcraft. Nevertheless, considering his humble origins and that he was self-educated, he did well to achieve a certain fame and immortality, especially in his native land. He was born in 1770 in the valley of Ettrick Water in a cottage now gone and is buried in the graveyard of Ettrick village parish church.

Three miles beyond the Loch o' the Lowes the road reaches the watershed and the Dumfriesshire border at a height of 1,100 feet, near where the waterfall known as the Grey Mare's Tail tumbles 200 feet into Moffat Water, thus ending the short journey of the wild foam-tossed Tail Burn which overflows from Loch Skene. The fall is Scottish National Trust property and is one of the highest in the country.

Ettrick Water rises on the slopes of Ettrick Pen (2,269 feet) and Capel Fell (2,223 feet) and flows north-eastwards to meet Yarrow Water through the heart of Ettrick Forest. The B709 from Langholme follows the Water all the way to Selkirk, both passing through the pleasant village of Ettrickbridge where David Steel, the present Leader of the Liberal Party, lives. Ettrick and Yarrow rival each other in scenic beauty and it would be invidious to choose between them.

Liberal Party leader, David Steel, M.P. for Roxburgh, Selkirk and Peebles.

CHAPTER EIGHT

Selkirk to Melrose

W E NOW come to the stretch of the Tweed associated with Sir Walter Scott and which will ever be the mecca of those who love and appreciate the works of this great Scottish novelist and poet.

Scott was born in his father's house in College Wynd, Edinburgh on the 15th August 1771, one of a family of twelve children, six of whom died in infancy. He was educated at the High School and University and in 1786 was apprenticed to his father who was Writer to the Signet. Walter was called to the Bar in 1792 but was never enthusiastic about law. On the 24th December 1797 he married at Carlisle, Margaret Charlotte Charpentier, daughter of Jean Charpentier of Lyons. The couple continued to live in Edinburgh, but when Walter was appointed Sheriff-Deputy of Selkirkshire in 1799 it became increasingly difficult for him to travel to and from the capital and so in 1804 they moved to "Ashiestiel" in the village of Caddenfoot. He rented the house from his cousins and probably spent there the happiest seven years of his life. Scott said of "Ashiestiel" that it was "A decent farmhouse overhanging the Tweed and situated in wild pastoral country", while Buchan referred to it as "Half farm, half manor".

Hereabouts the river flows through a deep, narrow and well wooded defile past the villages of Holylee, Caddenfoot, Fairnilee and Yair. Scott's favourite walk from "Ashiestiel" was to Elibank's ruined castle of the Murrays, seat of the Lords Elibank and the remains of a sixteenth century tower where Alison Rutherford, Mrs Patrick Cockburn, wrote "I've seen the smiling of Fortune beguiling" to the tune of "Flowers o' the Forest". Scott's opinion was that she wrote it after the financial disaster which ruined seven Selkirk lairds, or it may refer to the depopulation of Ettrick Forest.

The walk to Clovenfords was another favourite with Scott and there is a statue of him outside the inn which he used to frequent on his visits to the village. "Ashiestiel" was where his first literary attempts were made, beginning with translations from the German and the collecting and editing of old ballads. His first poem, "The Lay of the Last Minstrel", was published in 1805, followed by "Marmion" and "The Lady of the Lake". In 1806 he became a Clerk of the Court of Session and five years later bought Cartley Hole Farm for £4,000 from the Rev. Dr Robert Douglas of Galashiels. He named it

"Abbotsford" after the adjoining ford near the confluence of Gala Water with the Tweed and because all the surrounding land had once belonged to Melrose Abbey. When Scott bought the estate it was an un-drained water meadow and he affectionately referred to it as his "Clarty Hole".

Sir Walter Scott's statue in front of his "local" at Clovenfords.

In 1814 *Waverley* was published and proved such a success that other novels followed in rapid succession. He is said to have written the equivalent of thirty printed pages every day. In 1826, owing to the failure of two business ventures and the expense incurred in pulling down the farm and completing the building of the mansions between 1822 and 1824, he found himself in severe financial difficulties and in debt to the extent of £117,000. He at once undertook the task of paying off his creditors and by 1830 they had received £70,000 of the money he owed them but the great creative effort he put into the work brought on paralysis. This, coupled with lameness contracted as a result of a serious illness which he suffered when only eighteen months old, remained with him until his death on the 21st September 1832. Of all his poems "Marmion" perhaps takes first place and of his novels the most notable are *Guy Mannering, The Antiquary, Old Mortality, Rob Roy, Ivanhoe* and *The Heart of Midlothian.*

"Abbotsford" from across the Tweed.

Walter and his wife lived in the farm for seven years before their plans for enlarging it commenced in 1818. Finally in 1822 the old house was demolished and the "Abbotsford" of today completed two years later with Sir Walter, as he then was, having been created a baronet in 1820 by George IV, making many suggestions to the architects regarding its design and construction. For example he arranged for the setting in an upper wall of the house the lintel from the door of the Old Tolbooth in Edinburgh, "The Heart of Midlothian." This was presented by the city's magistrates to Scott after the Tolbooth was demolished in 1817. On the lintel are carved the words: —

"The Lord of armies is my Protector
Blessit are they that trust in the Lord, 1575"

The house, imposing rather than fine, in the sham-gothic and bastard-baronial style of its time, lies in a terraced situation above the river and apart from its association with the author is a veritable museum. It contains a fine collection of arms, armour and several thousand books acquired by the author. In the library there is also a case containing relics of Bonnie Prince Charlie, Flora Macdonald, Rob Roy, Robert Burns and Napoleon I. Among the treasures are Napoleon's pen case from Fontainebleau and his pistols, leather-bound blotter and cloak clasp of golden bees found in his carriage at Waterloo and personally collected from the battlefield by Scott. There is also Montrose's sword and a cabinet captured in his baggage after the battle of Philiphaugh; Rob Roy's purse, dirk, broadsword and gun; Bonnie Prince Charlie's quaigh or drinking cup, which has a glass bottom, so that the person drinking could guard against a surprise attack, and a lock of his hair. There is also Bonnie Dundee's pistol, a pocket-book worked by Flora Macdonald, Helen Macgregor's brooch, Burns' tumbler with some of his verses scratched upon it and many other items of great national and historic interest. The drawing room is hung with hand-painted Chinese wallpaper and there is a Portuguese ebony roll-top desk and matching chairs given to Sir Walter by George IV. The study has been left in very much the state it was at the time of Scott's death and contains his writing desk and chair, his death mask and a small desk made of wood from ships of the Spanish Armada. He died peacefully in bed in the dining room, to which he had been moved to be within sight and sound of his beloved Tweed.

On the outskirts of Galashiels, on the Edinburgh to Melrose road, a wall tablet records "At this spot, on his pathetic journey home to Abbotsford and his beloved Borderland, Sir Walter Scott, gazing on this scene for the last time, sprang up with a cry of delight, 11th July 1832." This was on his return from Rome whence he had gone in vain in an endeavour to recover his failing health. Scott's favourite view of the Eildon Hills and their wooded environs were passed by his funeral procession on its way from "Abbotsford" to Dryburgh Abbey and it is recorded that the author's old horse paused of its own volition at the spot as it had done on so many occasions when carrying Scott. He was laid to rest under a massive granite block on which is the inscription: —

Sir Walter Scott, Baronet
Died September 21, A.D. 1832
              Here
At the Feet of Walter Scott
              Lie
The Mortal Remains of
John Gibson Lockhart,
His son-in-law,
Biographer and Friend.
Born 14th June 1794
Died 25 November 1854.

Portrait of Sir Walter Scott.

Also buried there are Scott's wife and Lt. Col. Sir Walter Scott, the second and last baronet. Margaret predeceased the author by six years and they left four children, two boys and two girls.

◀ Sir Walter Scott's study at "Abbotsford."

Many interesting people stayed at "Abbotsford" as guests of Sir Walter, including Maria Edgeworth, Wordsworth, Thomas Moore and Washington Irving. After 1832 tourists went in increasing numbers year by year, 1,500, including 20 Americans, visiting the house the following year. On the 22nd August 1867 Queen Victoria had tea with the family and King George V and Queen Mary, accompanied by the Duke and Duchess of York, were visitors on the 12th July 1923.

The Eildon Hills which loomed so large in Scott's affection is really one hill with three peaks. According to legend the hill was cut into three parts by the devil when he was challenged to do so by Michael Scott, the wizard who lived from about 1175 to 1230, was a great scholar and is believed to have been buried at Melrose. Dante refers to Scott by condemning him to look backwards for his attempts to look into the future. Scott was a great traveller, spending many years on the continent and even associating with the French and Italian courts in Paris and Rome. Although never in holy orders he took advantage of one of the roles devolving on monasteries and other religious establishments by seeking shelter and sustenance under their roofs before finally returning home to Oakwood Tower near Selkirk. His reputation as a wizard and an associate of the devil seems to have originated from his interest in alchemy.

The Eildons is the site of the largest Roman camp in southern Scotland, the legionary station of Trimontium, which was excavated in 1908 and whose relics are now in the National Museum of Antiquities in Edinburgh. The Hills provide an easy climb and the reward of fine views from the top; Walter Scott averred that from the summit forty places "famous in war and verse" could be seen and the best view of Melrose can be achieved from the top of Mid Eildon at a height of 1,385 feet.

There is an old Border legend that King Arthur and his knights lie entombed in a vast cavern under the Eildons, after having waged relentless warfare in the area against advancing heathen hordes.

Perhaps the beauty of these hills is best expressed by the eighteenth century poet, Andrew Scott of Bowden: —

"O Eildon Hills, huge sisters three,
As fair you rise as ony,
Scotia has higher hills than thee,
But few gleam half as bonny."

To the other and more famous Scott, Sir Walter, the Eildons had special appeal and he often used to climb to the summit to admire the breathtaking views. On the summit of Mid Hill there is a granite block, erected in 1927 for the publicly subscribed sum of £140, on which is fixed a brass plate inscribed with the various points of interest that can be viewed from the top and with the dedication: —

"To the memory of Sir Walter Scott. From this spot he
was wont to view and point the glories of the Borderland".

"Abbotsford" and the Eildon Hills.

It is an interesting and unspoilt area for naturalists and in 1974 during a
survey by the local Support Group of the Scottish Wildlife Trust two hundred
and twenty-four species of flowering plants and ferns were recorded though
the Group considered that area for area the banks of the Tweed would
probably have produced as high as three hundred and fifty species. A wide
variety of animals, birds, butterflies and moths can also be found by those
prepared to devote time and patience to their investigations.

Galashiels derives its name from "gwala", a full stream, and "shiels" or
shelters, probably thatched cottages, on the banks of Gala Water and is
situated in the midst of fine rolling hills. The town became a burgh in 1864
and like several of its neighbours is a textile manufacturing centre with
woollen, tweed and hosiery mills, and the Scottish College of Textiles is

situated there. This is one of the most advanced establishments of its kind in the world and a mecca for aspiring textile leaders. It was the first Border town to attempt the commercial production of textiles on a big scale. For centuries more wool was produced in the Tweed valley than could be used locally and the surplus was exported to Flanders by the Abbots of Melrose who virtually had a monopoly of the trade. In the middle of the sixteenth century the Scottish Parliament decided to try to stop the export trade and encourage home manufacture, to which end Flemish weavers were persuaded to settle in the Borders. Tweed cloth has nothing to do with the river but got its name from the error of an English clerk reading the Scots word "tweels" or "twills" for "tweed". Like Moffat, the town has marked its dependence on wool with a statue symbolizing the connection, a shepherd carrying a ram on his shoulders. The clock tower of the Municipal Buildings was designed by Sir Robert Lorimer and standing in front of it is one of the finest war memorials in Scotland, a statue in bronze of a Border Reiver by Thomas Clapperton.

The burgh's flag includes the date 1503, commemorating the marriage of Margaret Tudor of England with James IV of Scotland and because Margaret was a descendant of the House of York and Lancaster the flag also has representations of white and red roses as well as the thistle. Ultimately the marriage of Margaret and James led to the union of the crowns of both countries a century later and their union was referred to as the "marriage of the rose and thistle". Margaret's dowry was the lands comprising Ettrick Forest and the marriage is commemorated annually at the end of "Braw Lads Week" in June in a ceremony known as the "mixing of the flowers".

The Braw Lads date back to 1337 when a party of English raiders were trapped in a grove of wild plum trees by the men of Galashiels and duly put to rout. Not only is this event remembered each year but is also represented in the town's coat of arms—a pair of foxes and the words "soor plums" interposed with the date of this famous local episode. Furthermore there is a boiled sweet called a Soor Ploom, a tart green concoction with a taste of lemon and lime—or a sour plum.

Along the hills west of Galashiels runs the Catrail, a defensive work attributed to the ancient Britons and originally consisting of a chain of forts connected by a deep fosse or rampart. The terminal fort was on Rink Hill which commands lovely views over Tweeddale.

Just north of Galashiels is the fifteenth century Boothwick Castle where Mary and Bothwell stayed in 1567 and were nearly captured by Morton, Mary escaping disguised as a page.

Buckholm Tower, now in ruins near the town, possesses an eighteenth century ghost in the person of its then owner, a man named Pringle who murdered two Covenanters, father and son, George and William Elliot. Covenanters were, of course, lawbreakers and Pringle used to hunt them down in the surrounding hills with packs of dogs. The Elliots had been captured and placed in a cell at Buckholm to await trial and there they were done to death by a drink-besotted Pringle who then forced the wife and mother to view the corpses of her husband and son: thereupon she put a curse on Pringle to the effect that the hounds of hell should pursue him day and night throughout eternity. From then onwards Pringle imagined himself being pursued and torn apart by ferocious hounds and soon he was driven insane and died, but the baying of hounds can still be heard on the anniversary of his death—or so it is said.

Two miles west of Melrose the Tweed is joined yet again by one of its many tributaries. The valley of Allan Water is green and pleasant and off the beaten track and with its Fairy Dene makes an enticing retreat on a hot summer's day. Now in deep shadow, now splashed with sunshine, the water ripples under rustic bridges and past banks lined with beeches and firs. At Allanfoot or Bridgend the Tweed was spanned in ancient times by an unusual wooden bridge, unusual because the keeper's house was built over a pier in mid-stream from where he could raise or lower the bridge to the left and right banks of the river. The bridge is described in Scott's "Monastery" as are the three towers, Glendearg, Langshaw and Colinslie, standing within a mile or so of each other at the head of the glen. Nearby is the peel tower of Darnick dating from 1425 and one of the few still happily well preserved. The term "peel tower" in this context is really a misnomer since "pele" refers to a timber palisade or stockade which enclosed or protected the house or tower of a Border laird and not a stone erection at all. The tower itself appears to have been given the name "pele" for the first time in the sixteenth century and its original meaning has vanished from general understanding.

Thomas Clapperton's "Border Reiver" in front of Sir Robert Lorimer's clock tower at Galashiels.

This section of the journey down river ends at Melrose, a town with the distinction of being the birthplace of the "seven-a-side" form of rugby. The rose red stone abbey was founded in 1136 by David I for the Cistercians, or Black Friars, from Rievaulx in North Yorkshire. They specialised in agriculture, fruit growing and animal breeding so it was natural for them to settle where meadowland was plentiful and the soil rich and where there was ample scope for development. Furthermore there were trout and salmon on hand ready for the taking. David was a fanatical builder of cathedrals and monasteries in which he installed English or French-speaking monks of the new, strictly disciplined orders. Holyrood was one of these establishments and in it he enshrined a piece of wood which Queen Margaret had believed to be a fragment of the true Cross or "holy rood". The abbey was burned by Edward II in 1322 when he also had killed Bruce's friend, the Abbot of Peebles and many of his monks because the Scots' scorched-earth policy had left his army hungry. Bruce immediately awarded £2,000 out of his treasury for the rebuilding and maintenance of the abbey. His heart is interred under the chancel's east window near the high altar, though his body is buried with that of his Queen, Elizabeth de Burgh, in Dunfermline Abbey. Bruce had instructed his friend, Sir James Douglas, to have his heart removed from his body at death and take it on a crusade to the Holy Land in payment of a vow he had made in one of his dire extremities and had been prevented from fulfilling in person. Douglas was killed on the crusade after casting the heart into the battle and plunging after it to his death. The heart was recovered from the battlefield and brought back to Melrose in fulfilment of Bruce's wish. Others buried in the abbey include Alexander II and his Queen Johanna, Michael Scott, the Eildon Wizard, and several members of the Douglas family.

Another famous name associated with the Abbey is that of Cuthbert, a Northumbrian shepherd boy who for some time was a monk at Melrose before becoming Prior and, later, Bishop of Lindisfarne. He died in 687 and his memory is revered in the famous Lindisfarne Gospels now in the British Museum; his remains lie behind the high altar of Durham Cathedral.

The abbey is rich in statuary despite the effects of the Reformation. Three statues are of particular interest, one being of a pig playing the bagpipes, another of a cook with a ladle and the third of the Virgin with the Child in her arms. The Child is headless and the story goes that when the head was struck off it fell on the arm of the desecrator, permantly disabling him. This effectively stopped any further destruction and the unfortunate man was known ever afterwards as "Stumpy" Thomson.

Architecturally the choir and nave are outstanding and the south transept window tracery is particularly fine; there is also an interesting museum for those with time to spare.

CHAPTER NINE

Melrose to Kelso

SIX miles south of Melrose, Dryburgh Abbey is magnificently situated in a bend of the river surrounded by lawns planted with a wide variety of fine trees, including Cedars of Lebanon reputedly brought back from the Crusades and a yew about eight hundred years old. In 1140 it was chosen by the Canons Regular of the Premonstratensian Order from Alnwick for their first house in Scotland. Dryburgh is a derivation of Darach Bruach, the bank or grove of the oaks, suggesting early occupation by Druid priests. It is also possible that St Modan, a disciple of St Columba, used it as a base for his missionary journeyings in the Borders since it is known that he was at the abbey in 522 and that he visited Dumfries, Falkirk, Roseneath, Stirling and Loch Etive.

Like so many other buildings in the area the abbey suffered severely at the hands of the English and it was badly damaged at least three times, the last occasion being in 1544. Nevertheless much remains of interest and beauty and it is now preserved by the Department of the Environment, having been given to the nation in 1919 by Lord Glenconner.

When Earl Haig died from a heart attack on the 29th January 1928 he was buried in St Mary's aisle close to the grave of Sir Walter Scott. Only three families have burial rights at the abbey, the third one being the Erskines. The Haigs have even longer connections with the Borders than the Scotts, the family being established at Bemersyde since the twelfth century. One of the great soldier's ancestors, Petrus de Haga, was a generous benefactor in the early days of the abbey's foundation and this long connection was sealed when Haig's friends and admirers presented the adjoining Bemersyde estate with its mansion and peel tower to him in grateful recognition of his outstanding war service. It was purchased from another branch of the family and the Earl enjoyed a happy, but all too short, number of years there with his family.

Douglas Haig was born on the 19th June 1861 at 24, Charlotte Square, Edinburgh, the youngest son of John Haig, a well-to-do whisky distiller and head of the firm still renowned all over the world for its famous product. The family was a large one comprising four girls and five boys, typical of the numbers expected in a Victorian household. Whisky literally ran in the family, because his sister, Henrietta, of whom he was especially fond and who became even closer to him after his parents' deaths within a year of one another when he was in his late teens, married William Jameson, another distiller of repute. Douglas attended Orwell House Preparatory School in Edinburgh and then went to Clifton College, Bristol, going on at the age of nineteen to read English at Brasenose College, Oxford. He was, however, determined on a military career and in February 1884 went to the Royal Military College, Sandhurst, from where he was commissioned into the 7th Hussars a year later. In February 1896 he was appointed to the Staff College at Camberley. He had a whirlwind romance with Dorothy Vivian, meeting, proposing and being accepted all in the space of three days. Dorothy was a Maid of Honour to Queen Alexandra and they met at Windsor Castle when Edward VII invited Haig to stay there during Ascot race week. They were married in the private chapel of Buckingham Palace on the 11th July 1905 and had two daughters, Alexandra born in March 1907 and Doria born in November 1908, and one son, the second Earl, born in March, 1918. Haig served in India, the Sudan and South Africa and was appointed Commander-in-Chief of the British forces on the Western Front late in 1915. At the end of the war an Earldom was conferred on him and he was given a gratuity of £100,000.

Light shade on Dryburgh Abbey, resting place of Field Marshal Earl Haig of Bemersyde and Sir Walter Scott.

On a hill behind the abbey is a large statue of William Wallace, made by John Smith of Darnick in the early nineteenth century, so Dryburgh is very much associated with personalities who have played important parts in the long history of Scotland.

Close by the abbey is the town of St Boswell, named after the saint to whom Bede referred as "a priest of great virtue and of a prophetic spirit". A couple of miles outside the town is the early eighteenth century Mertoun House, seat of the Duke of Sutherland.

The ruins of Littledean Tower are also near the town. They are reputed to be the setting of a murder by a ghostly hand, a murder fortunately to be one of few regrets for the victim was to say the least an undesirable character. The story goes that the laird was an incorrigible drinker and wife beater and it was during one of his reprehensible outbursts that he declared in front of his drinking pals that a devil from hell would make a better lover and wife than his own spouse. In order to get over the effects of the evening's drinking the laird decided to go for a ride on his horse but was overtaken by a thunderstorm and torrential rain so that he sought shelter in a nearby cottage which he found to be occupied by a most attractive young lady. For a time the two met secretly in a wood and eventually became lovers, but soon the laird's wife came to know of the clandestine affair and decided to put a stop to it with the aid of some friends. The wood was duly surrounded and systematically searched but all that was found were some birds and a hare which rapidly took evading action. However, that night when the laird was returning home from one of his drunken revelries, a group of hares appeared and started to chase the frightened horse, one imagines in best Tam o' Shanter style. The laird thrashed around with his sword in an effort to dispose of the hares though this would appear to have been a futile exercise from the back of a horse; nevertheless he did succeed in striking off a paw of one of the hares and by some remarkable mischance it fell into his pocket. By this time man, horse and hares had arrived at the witches' local trysting place of Midlem and the hares abandoned their harassment and pursuit. Eventually the frightened laird arrived home and, to prove his extraordinary story to his wife, decided to show her the paw. On going to his pocket he found the paw had changed into a female hand which he hastily threw into the river, having weighted it with a stone. On his way back to the Tower yet another unnerving sight confronted him because there in the wood he could see his lover who had now not only turned into an old woman but was minus a hand. On arrival home the hand was there waiting for him so in desperation he threw it on the fire and saw it consumed by the flames. Next day he was found dead in front of the fire with his throat bearing every sign of strangulation!

Near Dryburgh there is a great bend in the river where it receives Leader Water coming down from the north. Near the village of Earlston on this tributary are the remains of the residence of Sir Thomas Learmonth, a prophetic poet known as Thomas the Rhymer or Thomas of Ercildoune, who was born in 1220 and died in 1297. He was a believer in the supernatural and was the writer of the story of a seven-year journey to Elfland. He was closely associated with Peter Haig of Bemersyde between 1250 and 1260 and responsible for the well known couplet: —

"Tide, tide, whate'er betide,
Haig will be Haig of Bemersyde."

Evening comes to Kelso; the river spanned by John Rennie's masterpiece with the Abbey rising above the north end.

Many of his prophecies are known to have come true and certainly his utterance about the Haig family has proved remarkably relevant even at a distance of some seven hundred years.

Higher up Leader Water is the royal burgh of Lauder, the only one in the county and with a population of only five hundred and seventy. Just outside the town is Thirlestane Castle, one of the country's oldest castles and the seat of the Maitlands, Earls of Lauderdale. It is a splendid turreted and towered manor house with fine gardens. Until the seventeenth century it was merely a Border tower, little different from its many neighbours, but it was transformed by the then Earl and his second wife, Bessie Dysart, reputedly Cromwell's mistress. This intimate relationship with the Protector proved vital to the saving of her future husband's life after the Battle of Worcester. He had been taken prisoner and faced possible execution but Bessie used her influence over Cromwell to advantage and he was pardoned. Twenty years later she married the Earl after the death of his first wife, and that same year a dukedom was conferred by Charles II, of whose notorious "Cabal" the Duke was the last named member. As with so many other places and houses in the Borders the name of Bonnie Prince Charlie is connected with Thirlstane because the Young Pretender stayed there after the battle of Prestonpans in 1745.

Back on the main river a mile or two beyond Rutherford the Tweed begins the first of two north-ward direction changes that bring it to Kelso through fine wooded scenery which compensates for the hills being left behind. Also on this reach there is a spectacular section at Makerstown where the river flings itself through a magnificent chasm, the water being churned into foam by the rocks.

Kelso, derived from "Calch" indicating lime and "How" meaning an elevated place, is situated in the Middle March, a low-lying area where the Teviot joins the Tweed. This market town faces south across the green plain towards the Cheviots and is most attractive and atypical of the Borderland. Its Flemish style cobbled market square contrasts delightfully with narrow streets and wynds and many appealing houses. The splendid five-arch bridge over the Tweed was designed by Rennie and completed in 1803, replacing one which collapsed during a flood six years previously, a disaster witnessed by thousands of people who had gathered hours before it fell once it had become known that serious cracks had appeared in the structure. The government paid £15,000 for Rennie's bridge but this had to be repaid over a period of years by the levying of a toll on all who made use of the structure. The tolls have long since been abolished but the classical toll-house still stands at the town-end of the bridge. Rennie put his Kelso design to good use since it became a model for London's Waterloo Bridge completed in 1817. Indeed when this was demolished two of its iron lampstandards were taken to Kelso for erection, thus cementing the affinity of the designer and his two creations.

Kelso Abbey in the light of the setting sun.

Kelso Abbey was at one time probably the greatest of the four Border abbeys. Benedictine monks from Tircon in Picardy settled in Selkirk in 1113 but within fifteen years decided Kelso would be a better site for their abbey than the steep hill above Ettrick Water that they had originally chosen for its foundation and in this move they had the blessing of David I. The abbey became very wealthy, possessing revenues from thirty-three parishes, many farms, manors, granges and fishing rights and the fines and forfeitures of Berwick county and town. Its abbots held premier status in the south until 1430 when they were superseded by those of St Andrews. They were the first ecclesiastics on the parliamentary roll and often performed the role of ambassador. The abbey was used as a fortress in 1545 when the town was attacked by the Earl of Hertford and after it fell the garrison, including twelve monks, was slaughtered. As with the neighbouring abbeys, time and depredation have left their mark but still remaining are a beautiful doorway, two fine arches and the facade of the north west transept.

74

Walter Scott attended Kelso Old Grammar School in 1783 and here he met fellow pupil James Ballantyne, who was destined to open a printing and publishing business with his brother in which the author was to invest heavily with disastrous results to himself, even though the brothers did publish most of his works.

Two miles north west across the river stands magnificent Floors Castle, a battlemented place designed by William Adam in 1721 and extended by Playfair in 1841, and which Walter Scott referred to as "altogether a kingdom for Oberon and Titania to dwell in". It is the seat of the Duke and Duchess of Roxburgh, has a window for each day of the year, contains pictures by Canaletto, Gainsborough, Lely, Raeburn, Reynolds and Wilson, a Victorian bird collection and fine porcelain, silver, tapestries and English and French furniture. It stands amidst beautiful gardens with splendid views of the Tweed in the valley below.

The magnificence of Floors Castle in its parkland setting with the river in the foreground.

It was in 1616 that Sir Robert Ker of Cessford was created the first Earl of Roxburgh and the Dukedom was conferred on the fifth Earl with the secondary title of Marquis of Bowmont which is borne by the Duke's heir. The present Duke is tenth in line and he married in 1977 Lady Jane Grosvenor, younger daughter of the fifth Duke of Westminster. The family name of Innes Ker came by marriage in the late seventeenth century and it was Sir James Innes Ker, the sixth Baronet who succeeded as the fifth Duke in 1812.

Six miles north west of Kelso yet another peel tower is situated. The 57 feet high Smailholm Tower, also known as Sandyknowe from the whin and volcanic outcrop on which it stands and a nearby farm of that name, once tenanted by Walter Scott's grandfather, was built in the sixteenth century by the Pringles. It passed into the Scotts of Harden family early in the seventeenth century and was frequently visited by the famous author from childhood when he stayed at his grandfather's farm; the tower is referred to in "Marmion" and "The Eve of St. John", and is an outstanding example of its kind with wonderful views of the distant countryside and, below, a delightful lochan. In Smailholm Church there is a memorial window to Scott who returned for a last visit to the farm and tower only a year before he died, accompanied by no less a person than J. M. W. Turner, the famous artist.

It is now necessary to tear ourselves away from the Tweed for a while so that we can follow upstream its longest and most important tributary, the Teviot, which is 37 miles long from its confluence with the Tweed to its source at Teviothead, nine miles above Hawick. The river flows in a rocky bed and for several miles its banks are bare of trees, though there is a delightful wooded stretch above Branxholm. The dale is not as broad as Tweeddale and is certainly wilder though fair and sylvan for all that.

Barely a mile upstream is the village of Roxburgh, situated on the site of one of the four royal burghs of Scotland of which virtually no trace remains except high green banks and scattered humps of masonry between the two rivers. Looking at the site today it is hard to imagine what it was like centuries ago when it was one of the mightiest royal fortresses in either England or Scotland with its royal mint, three churches, convent, schools and so many houses that as early as the twelfth century a new town had to be constructed to accommodate all the populace. Like so many other parts of the Borders the town suffered terribly from the depredations of the English and it was constantly changing hands, first occupied by the Scots, then by the English and then again by the Scots with bewildering regularity, though between 1300 and 1460 it was held continuously by English forces. It was on Edward I's personal command that Robert Bruce's sister, Mary, was hung in a cage in the castle from 1306-10 and here it was that James II of Scotland was killed by an exploding cannon, known as "the Lion" and similar to the famous Mons Meg, during an attempt to capture the castle from the hated English enemy on the

3rd August 1460; a holly tree marks the spot in the grounds of Floors Castle where the king met his death. This accident occurred because of the king's interest in mechanical contrivances, an interest he had inherited from his father, and he frequently enjoyed himself by operating the great siege pieces with his own hands, but on this occasion with fatal results. The siege was, however, successful and James' widowed Queen, Mary of Gueldres, had the stronghold pulled down though it was rebuilt by the English in 1547. Now it has all vanished without trace and nothing remains of the former royal burgh's greatness. The nine year old son of James and Mary was crowned James III in Kelso Abbey soon after his father's death. It was at the castle that the no doubt apochryphal story originated of the wife of an English soldier lulling her child to sleep with the topical words: —

"Hush yet, hush ye, little pet ye,
Hush ye, hush ye, do not fret ye,
The Black Douglas shall not get ye."

From out of the darkness a hand came and rested on her shoulder, and a voice said "I'm not so sure of that". It was the notorious Sir James (Black) Douglas.

Many tales are told in the Borders about the Douglases, their hard fighting qualities, their callousness and their ruthlessness. The family's ancestral home was Douglas Castle, Walter Scott's "Castle Dangerous" and here they lived in considerable style. The James Douglas of the soldier's wife's tale was one of Robert Bruce's chief supporters and on Palm Sunday, 1307, an English force was trapped in St Bride's Chapel and massacred as they worshipped, whereupon Douglas and his companions sat down and ate the meal prepared for the unfortunate Englishmen.

Another kinsman of Sir James had the offensive habit of inviting his acquaintances to dinner and after wining and dining them, suggesting that they should transfer their properties to him. Those that demurred and refused to comply were hanged from a tree outside his bedroom window; this was done to remind himself "of the dangers of over indulgence" and to preserve his guests from the consequences of the morning after the night before!

The Percys of Alnwick were the Douglases' chief opponents and their most notable encounter was at the Battle of Otterburn in 1388. The Douglas was mortally wounded by the forces of Sir Henry Percy, Shakespeare's Hotspur, and as he lay dying quoted an ancient prophecy to his retainers: —

"I had a dream, a dreary dream,
Beyond the Isle of Skye,
I saw a dead man win a fight,
And I think that man was I."

Sure enough Scottish reinforcements appeared on the scene and the English force was swept aside.

The cobbled Market Square of Kelso.

Memories of fratricide between the Scots and English are all too frequently apparent as the Tweed and its feeder streams hurry along to the sea, but above the village of Nisbet is a reminder of one of the battles that was fought by the united countries against the French in 1815. On the summit of 741 feet high Peniel Heugh is a towering landmark erected by the Marquis of Lothian and his tenants to commemorate Wellington's victory at Waterloo. Just below the monument is Monteviot Park, a woodland estate where a number of craftsmen are busy demonstrating that the art of working in timber is far from moribund and, close by at Bonjedward, is situated the Borders Craft Centre, established by Lothian Estates, where Jed Water joins the Teviot. The estate is the ancestral home of the Marquis of Lothian whose son and heir is the Earl of Ancrum. The marquis is descended from Mark Ker of Cessford, who was created Earl of Lothian in 1606. Philip Ker, the eleventh Marquis, had a distinguished political career, being a Liberal member of Ramsey MacDonald's cabinet, holding office as Chancellor of the Duchy of Lancaster and Under Secretary of State for India and then ambassador to the United States of America in 1939-40. The Americans thought highly of him and when he died in Washington on the 12th December 1940 he was accorded a state funeral and buried in Arlington National Cemetery. The present Marquis has followed in the footsteps of his predecessor, having been a delegate to the United Nations General Assemby, the Council of Europe and Western European Union, as well as holding a succession of parliamentary offices.

The mansion dates from the sixteenth century with seventeenth century additions and is typically French in style, having shot holes, heraldic decorations, a circular stair-turret, conical angle turrets and a massive projecting chimney stack to the large flues and fireplace in the hall. Scott and William and Dorothy Wordsworth visited the house in September 1803 and no doubt took delight in the village which is quite charming with its green and the thirteenth century cross.

Between Ancrum and Hawick is the Earl of Minto's seat, Minto House, built in 1814. Scott was a regular visitor and there Thomas Campbell wrote "Lochiel's Warning". Perhaps the house's main interest, however, belongs to its predecessor on the same site because it was the birthplace in 1727 of Jane Elliot who wrote "Flowers o' the Forest". She was the daughter of Sir Gilbert Elliott, an ancestor of the Earls of Minto. Near Minto, in the little village of Denholm, were born two of Scotland's greatest linguists, Dr John Leyden (1775-1811) whose thatched cottage birthplace can still be seen, and Sir James A. H. Murray (1837-1915), the latter being editor of the New Oxford English Dictionary and whose birthplace is on the opposite side of the village green to that of Leyden. Denholm is a delightful village built round a large green in the centre of which is a monument to Leyden. By any standards he must have been a remarkable man especially so as he was born of poor parents with limited education. His father was a grieve, or farm manager, for a more prosperous relation and the family lived in a lonely cottage at Henlawshiel, under Rubislaw. John's grandmother taught him to read and he went to school at Kirkton which meant long hours of walking often in the bitterest of weather conditions. Fortunately the minister of Denholm was proficient in Greek and Latin and he helped John to acquire sufficient knowledge of the classics to obtain a place at Edinburgh University. Eventually he mastered and became proficient not only in Greek and Latin but also in Oriental languages, French, German, Hebrew, Icelandic, Italian and Spanish. After leaving University he wrote and tutored and then changed career by qualifying in medicine and surgery, going in 1803 to India as assistant-surgeon in Madras. Two years later he became Professor of Hindustani in Calcutta, where he became Assay-Master of the Mint, a commissioner and a judge. Later he went to Mysore as a consultant in geology, natural history and surgery with the commissioners. This remarkable and versatile man died of fever contracted on an expedition to Java with Lord Minto, having crammed into his short life of thirty-six years a staggering variety of professionalism and intellect which must surely be practically impossible to surpass.

On nearby Minto Crags are the ruins of the sixteenth century Fatlips Castle. This was formerly a stronghold of the Turnbull family, and a prominent landmark overlooking Teviotdale.

Hawick is the largest of the Border towns, the derivation being from the Anglo-Saxon "Haga" meaning place of safety and "Wic" a dwelling, and has a personal connection with the author of this book since his paternal grand-father was born in the town in 1882. In the museum and art gallery is a section dealing with the hosiery and woollen trade, the quality of the local products being of worldwide repute. One of the oldest Border Common Ridings is held each year in early June, lasts two days and celebrates the victory of local "callants" (youths) in 1514 over an English force at Hornshole Bridge, 2½ miles outside the town. A permanent memorial to this event is the horse monument in High Street.

Signs of industry at Hawick.

Hawick cannot boast of much by way of antiquarian history and it was only a village of one hundred and ten houses when Mary Queen of Scots confirmed a baronial charter. However, there is one particular feature of note, a large earthworks 312 feet in circumference and 30 feet high situated on high ground in a small park overlooking the Teviot and known locally as the Moat. Mounds such as this were frequently erected between the twelfth and fourteenth centuries for the purpose of having motte-and-bailey castles built on them. These erections were constructed by the border barons before stone castles became the more usual form of defence and consisted of a timber palisade surrounding a wooden castle covered with clay to prevent it being set on fire by blazing arrows. The Teviot flows through the town centre and is joined by the Slitrig which has several mills built over it on bridges. Like Berwick, Galashiels and Jedburgh the town lends its name to boiled spicy sweets of varying colour and shape called Hawick Balls.

Not far from Hawick is Hermitage Castle, one of the grimmest, largest and best preserved in the Borders. It was founded in 1244 and has been the scene of many historic incidents. Its four towers with 7 feet thick connecting walls have stood the ravages of time and are situated above Hermitage Water, named after a hermit's cell the remains of which can still be identified close to the castle. It stands four square at the head of Liddesdale Valley, flanked by two small streams, Castle Sike and Lady's Sike, and has been referred to as "the guardhouse of the bloodiest valley in Britain". The earliest holders were the family of Soulis, one of whom, Lord William, was a most despicable and undesirable character. He treated the peasantry in a most deplorable manner and his more noble neighbours even worse, having the habit of arranging their murder after inviting them to the castle in the guise of friendship. It is said that one of these unfortunate nobles, the Count of Kielder, was drowned in one of the nearby streams after accompanying Lord William on a hunting foray and being wined and dined at the castle.

Soulis was such a bad individual that he had no difficulty in selling his soul to the Devil and the latter returns every seven years to open up the chamber beneath the ruins where the bargain was transacted, having been provided with the key by Sir William when he left the castle for the last time. This occurred as a result of the king, so disgusted by his evil ways, ordering his retainers to "boil him and sup his broo". This was enthusiastically executed by wrapping William in sheet lead and boiling him in a huge cauldron inside a druid circle near the castle.

Eventually the castle came into the possession of the Douglas family, who apparently were no better than their predecessors. Sir William Douglas had a friend, Sir Alexander Ramsay of Dalhousie, who was appointed Sheriff of Teviotdale much to the disgust and envy of Sir William who, accompanied by a body of armed vassals, forced his way into the court at Hawick in 1342,

The forbidding ruins of Hermitage Castle in its wild moorland setting near Hawick.

seized the sheriff and cast him and his horse into a dungeon where they starved to death. What the poor horse had to do with the matter is difficult to comprehend but at the end of the eighteenth century the bones of a horse and man and parts of a bridle and saddle were discovered under the castle. Ramsay is supposed to have taken seventeen days to expire, rather longer than anticipated, because the dungeon was situated beneath the granary and he was able to survive for a time by eating the grain which trickled through the floor.

Perhaps the castle's most interesting period occurred in the sixteenth century when James Hepburn, Earl of Bothwell, was appointed Lieutenant of the Marches and Keeper of Liddesdale in 1566; these appointments conferred on the holder the occupancy of the castle. In October of that year the Earl and his troops set out to capture or kill Jock Elliott of the Park, a notorious freebooter. Elliott had quite a following and there was something of a battle before the forces of law and order gained the upper hand and it was in the course of the skirmish that Bothwell shot Elliott in the thigh. Elliott fell and Bothwell, believing him to be either dead or severely wounded, went up to him and for his temerity was severely injured when he was stabbed three times by Elliott. When word of Bothwell's injuries was given to Mary Queen of Scots, when staying in Jedburgh where she was holding assizes, she made the fifty-miles return ride to visit him at the castle. She accomplished the journey in a single day and as a result fell desperately ill of a fever from which she nearly died. Much more recently the ruins have been used as film settings, including "Macbeth" and "Mary, Queen of Scots".

82

Between Hawick and Teviothead is the village of Branxholme which was the principal setting for "The Lay of the Last Minstrel". The castle is the property of the Duke of Buccleuch, the original building being burned by the Earl of Northumberland in 1532 and subsequently rebuilt on a smaller scale.

Three miles to the north, set romantically above a deep ravine of Borthwick Water is Harden House, a plain crowstepped-gabled house of the seventeenth century, the ancestral home of the Scotts of Harden. The present house replaced an earlier stronghold destroyed about 1590 after the Scotts had gained the property in 1501 from Lord Home. The famous freebooter, Auld Wat of Harden, was a member of the Scott family who married the "Flower of Yarrow" of ballad fame. The cattle that he rustled were kept in the deep glen below the house and it is said that when the beef supply was running short his wife placed on the table a covered dish which revealed, when the cover was lifted, a pair of spurs. This was a sign for Auld Wat to get back to the business of rustling a few more cattle. His son, rather obviously known as Young Wat, was the hero of one of the most romantic tales of the Border country. The scene is set high on the Tweed's south bank below Walkerburn in the now ruined tower of Elibank Castle, once the home of Muckle-moued Meg, who reputedly had such a large mouth that prospective suitors were driven away without waiting for a second look. Meg was the daughter of Sir Gideon Murray who took possession of Elibank in 1594 and the other participant of the romance was Young Wat who was caught stealing Sir Gideon's cattle. He was given the choice of marriage to Meg or to be hanged. He chose to hang but at the last moment changed his mind after catching sight, it is said, of a tear in Meg's eye. As in all good romances the couple were married and lived happily ever after.

"That day they were wedded, that night they were bedded,
An' Juden has feasted them gaily an' free;
But aft the bridegroom has he rallied an' bladded,
What faces he made at the big hanging tree."

It is not recorded whether Young Wat continued to rustle his, now, father-in-law's cattle.

Sadly all this is fanciful and stems from the imaginings of Sir Walter Scott and James Hogg. The facts of the case are that a marriage contract was agreed, amicably so far as is known, on the 18th February, 1611 and the couple were married on the 1st May of the same year.

Teviot has several other tributaries in addition to those already mentioned, receiving the waters of Ale, Kale, Rule and Allan as it flows down from the hills to the parent river. Ale Water is rather curiously named as Ale is derived from the ancient word Aln, meaning water, and thus we have the curious anomaly of Ale Water having the connotation of Water Water!

The massive ruins of Cessford Castle a mile or two on the south bank of Kale Water was once the seat of the Kers, later Innes Ker, Innes being the name of descendants of the female line and whose chief is the Duke of Roxburgh.

Jedburgh is the county town of Roxburghshire, a royal burgh appropriately situated on Jed Water. David I founded a priory there in 1118 for the Canons Regular of Beauvais in Francis; twenty-nine years later it was raised to abbey status. It is the most complete of all the Border monastic houses — "the most perfect and beautiful example of the Saxon and early Gothic in Scotland". The transept tower is 86 feet high and there are three tiers of arches forming the nave arcading, triforium and clerestory, an elaborately carved Norman doorway and a rose window known as St Catherine's Wheel. The abbey was destroyed on Henry VIII's orders because the Scots refused to the betrothal of Mary Queen of Scots with Edward VI. It was subsequently rebuilt and in use until 1873.

On the 7th October 1566 Mary, accompanied by her nobles, left Edinburgh for Jedburgh, where they arrrived two days later. The purpose of the visit was to hold a Justice Ayres or Circuit Court in a building, now demolished, in the Canongate. Mary at first stayed at the *Spread Eagle Hotel* in High Street, which is one of the oldest hostelries in the country. However, due to a fire, she was forced to look for alternative accommodation and this she found in what is now known as Queen Mary's House. This is a "bastel house", one of a series of six fortified dwellings, of which it is the only survivor. They were built expressly for the purpose of repelling potential invaders of the family hearth. It was in this house that she recovered from the illness contracted as a result of her horse ride to see the wounded Bothwell at Hermitage Castle. A number of relics are on display in the house, including Mary's communion set, a shoe from her pony, a tapestry which she worked and her death mask. There are also her watch and thimble-case, both of which were found in unusual circumstances. The watch was uncovered by a mole in 1817 in boggy ground near Hawick, obviously having been lost during the notorious ride. The thimble-case had been left at the farmhouse of Barnes in the same area, where Mary had stopped to repair her dress. Also on display is the Great Seal of Scotland.

A rare feature of the house is the staircase leading from the Queen's bedroom down to the dining room. It has a left-hand twist instead of the more usual right-handed one and this is supposed to be due to the fact that the Ker family, who owned the building for several centuries, were a left-handed clan. The leftwards twist enabled them to use their left sword-arm to repel unwelcome guests. Sir James Barrie officially opened the house in 1929 and was made a Freeman of the burgh on the same day.

Queen Mary's house,
Jedburgh.

Sir Walter Scott made his first appearance as an advocate at the Court House in 1793 and later sat on the bench as Sheriff; he also entertained William and Dorothy Wordsworth in a house in The Bow. Robert Burns was made a Freeman of the town, which was the first to recognise his great poetic ability. Mary Somerville, the noted mathematician and founder of Somerville College, Oxford was born in the town as was the eminent optical inventor and scientist, Sir David Brewster. After spending a night in the town Bonnie Prince Charlie led his army into England in 1745, to brief success and eventual rout.

Jedburgh Castle, now a museum illustrating the early nineteenth century penal system, was built in 1823, originally for use as the county jail: other interesting structures are the delightful three-arched Auld Brig and nearby sixteenth century Ferniehurst Castle, now used as a youth hostel but originally the seat of the Kers who for many years were Wardens of the Middle and Eastern Marches. Near the castle is the last remnant of the ancient and extensive Jed Forest; known as the Capon Tree it stands on the bank of the river where it is crossed by the main road to the south, the ageing branches being carefully supported to prevent them breaking off from the trunk.

In the town after Alexander III's second marriage in 1285 a masque was staged in honour of the nuptials and in the presence of the royal family and a goodly number of the nobility of the borders. The merriment and festivities were at their height when to the assembly's horror and amazement a skeleton appeared and danced before the king prior to threading its way through the ranks of the guests and vanishing. Everyone shrank back from this frightening apparition and most agreed that it was an appearance of ill-omen and sure enough, less than six months later, the king met a violent end falling off a horse and breaking his neck. The Borders is an area much given to deeds of the supernatural, fairies, witches, the doings of the devil and such like so this story might be, it may be thought, cast in the illusory mould of most of the others but not so — it is well attested and recorded.

Jedburgh no doubt strongly refutes Melrose's claim to be the originator of seven-a-side rugby and shares a distinction with some of its neighbours of having an item to eat named after it; this is a dark-brown toffee delicately flavoured with peppermint and curled into the shape of a snail — hence Jethart Snails.

Seven miles south east of Kelso are the twin villages of Yetholm and Kirk Yetholm, divided by Bowmont Water and right on the border with England and the end of the Pennine Way. The Yetholms are the capital of the Scots gypsies with such down to earth names as Blyth, Brown and Gordon, and the home of the great Romany family of Faa, who were notable smugglers, goods from the Northumbrian coast frequently finding their way into Scotland via this area. Apart from smuggling the gypsies were involved in more honest ways of earning a living, such as traditional tinkering and the carrying of coal to the Border towns, though how much this honest trading was merely a cover for the smuggling only the gypsies themselves could say and presumably prudence prevented them from doing too much of the telling. When Auld Will Faa died at Coldstream in 1847 many hundreds of his followers walking, or riding on donkeys or ponies, accompanied the corpse to Kirk Yetholm where it was ceremoniously interred in the churchyard. Will was succeeded by Charlie Blyth and when he died there was no male issue so the succession had to devolve on one of his two daughters; Esther was the elder but her father wished Ellen to follow him as queen. This created something of a problem so it was decided to settle the matter in accordance with Romany law, that is by combat between the two contestants. Esther emerged victorious from the ensuing wrestling bout on the green at Kirk Yetholm and she was proclaimed "Esther Faa Blyth Rutherford, Queen of all the Gypsies in the Northern Kingdom — challenge who dare". In 1898 the coronation of Charles Faa Blyth attracted thousands of spectators but, Gypsy King though he was, his palace was nothing more than a but-and-ben (two roomed) cottage which can still be seen. Gypsies are a fraternity not generally liked by the less nomadic members of our society and are indeed frequently feared as they probably have been for hundreds of years. Fortunately these days gypsies are treated no differently from the rest of us when they have been found guilty of breaking the law and certainly more humanely than was the case recorded at Jedburgh in May 1714. A group of ten gypsies were accused of setting fire to a house and though three were acquitted five others were deported. The two ringleaders, Janet Stewart and Patrick Faa of Kirk Yetholm, were whipped through the streets of the town and Janet had to stand at the Market Cross with her ear nailed to a post. Patrick's treatment was even more drastic since both his ears were cut off and he was transported for life to America.

Newark Castle.

CHAPTER TEN

Kelso to Coldstream

ABOUT half way between Kelso and Coldstream the Tweed is joined by Eden Water flowing down from the north. In its higher reaches it passes close to another fine border mansion, Mellerstain House, built by William and Robert Adam between 1725 and 1765 and the home of Lord Binning, son and heir of the Earl of Haddington, family name Baillie-Hamilton. There is not much doubt that this is Scotland's most famous Adam house standing like its near neighbour, Floors Castle, in fine gardens with a magnificent view across the lake to the Cheviots. The ceilings are particularly noteworthy, that of the library being one of Robert Adam's greatest works, dating from 1773. The genius of the Adam father and son alliance is complemented by great names in the history of art and furniture — Bassano, Birley, Constable, Gainsborough, Kneller, Maes, Raeburn, Ramsay, Van Dyke, Chippendale and Sheraton. The house is also noteworthy for its tapestries and eighteenth century wallpaper and garments, to say nothing of Bonnie Prince Charlie's bagpipes.

Mellerstain House, finest of Adam houses.

On the opposite bank to Mellerstain near Greenlaw are the ruins of thirteenth century Hume Castle standing on top of a hill. Its long and chequered history includes its capture by Somerset in 1547, its recapture two years later by the Earl of Hume, its fall to Sussex in 1569 and its capitulation to Cromwell in 1651. The castle was razed to the ground but in 1794 the Earl of Marchmont restored it as a "sham antique" complete with battlemented walls.

Lower downstream Eden Water flows past the village of Ednam, the birthplace in 1700 of James Thomson, who wrote the words of "Rule Britannia" and in 1793 of Henry Francis Lyte, the author of "Abide with Me" and "Praise my Soul, the King of Heaven." Thomson is commemorated by an obelisk set on a mound on the Kelso road but Lyte is best remembered by the two immortal hymns he wrote, hymns that have comforted and inspired countless thousands of people in a wide variety of exultation and pageantry, danger and stress. "Praise my Soul" was published in 1834 when Lyte was rector of Brixham, the words being based on the 103rd Psalm; the centenary of his death coincided with the marriage of Her Majesty the Queen and His Royal Highness the Duke of Edinburgh on the 20th November 1947 and most appropriately the hymn was sung at the splendid ceremony in Westminster Abbey. It is the hymn almost certainly chosen more often than any other to be sung on important joyful national occasions.

"Abide with Me" has, of course, quite a different connotation and has found both deep outward and inward expression in circumstances of great trial and tribulation as well as being sung for many years in the unlikely setting of Wembley Stadium at F.A. Cup Finals. Prisoners of war have found it a great comfort and many have witnessed to the fact that they have felt nearer to homes and loved ones when it was sung than at any other time of their incarceration. It gave comfort and strength to Nurse Edith Cavell in 1916 as she prepared to face a German firing squad in Brussels; it was sung by the passengers of the ill-fated *Titanic* as it foundered in the Atlantic on the 14th April, 1912 and it gave solace to the famous explorer, Sir Ernest Shackleton, as he lay hopefully awaiting rescue in the isolation of an Antarctic winter. Lyte trained for the ministry in Dublin and went as a curate to Marazion in Cornwall before moving to Brixham where he came much in contact with the fishermen of the port and the ever present dangers they faced in their calling and it may well have been this that gave him the inspiration to write his memorable words; he died and was laid to rest in Nice whence he had gone to avoid the vagaries of an English winter. In case Lyte should be thought of only a two-timer hymn writer it must be remembered that he also wrote "God of mercy, God of grace", based on Psalm 67, "Pleasant are Thy courts above", based on Psalm 84, "Far from my heavenly home" and "Jesus, I my cross have taken".

Two miles below the confluence with Eden Water the Tweed begins to flow south of the border at Carham and then soon reaches Coldstream, a clean, narrow but long little town. Here the Tweed is joined by Leet Water and flows delightfully between woodlands and green banks. Just before reaching Coldstream the borders take a loop inland to the south leaving the river for almost half a mile and thereby enclosing in Scotland a portion of land below the Weir of Lees which seemingly should be in England.

General George Monck, erstwhile Cromwellian and latterday restorer of the Stuart's fortunes.

Coldstream is, of course, always associated with the second oldest regiment of Foot Guards in the British Army but contrary to most people's beliefs the regiment was not raised in the town. It had been in existence for ten years as part of the Commonwealth Army when the first Commander, General Monck, established his headquarters at Coldstream in December, 1659, having formed the unit out of Fenwick's and Heselrige's Regiments in 1650 to fight Scottish Presbyterians. The new regiment recruited mainly local men who showed more allegiance to their Commanding Officer than to Cromwell for when Monck changed sides and captured Newcastle on behalf of the King and helped in the restoration of Charles II they followed him, such was their liking of the man and his popularity with them. The regiment had its Headquarters in the Market Square and the Guards' House is now a museum with a plaque above the entrance presented by the Guards when they received the freedom of the town on the 10th August 1968, confirming Monck's departure for London on 1st January 1660 to restore Charles II to the throne. The Coldstream appellation was originally a nickname of sorts which eventually stuck and is now remembered with pride by all who serve or have served with the famous regiment; it is synonymous with the courage and precision associated with the Brigade of Guards.

90

John Smeaton's graceful bridge reflected in the quiet water at Coldstream.

Coldstream is situated on the north bank of the river and connected with the village of Cornhill on the English side by a beautiful stone seven-arched bridge built by John Smeaton of Eddystone Lighthouse fame between 1763 and 1766. The design is somewhat unusual in that there are a series of dummy flood openings above the main piers. The red tiled toll-house at the Coldstream end of the bridge was once notorious for runaway marriages, rivalling the famous smithy at Gretna Green. The tale is told of a would-be bridegroom shooting at a pursuer's horse at Cornhill in order to give himself more time for marrying across the river. Perhaps the most remarkable thing about the marriage business was that the Lords Eldon, Erskine and Broughton of their day married in this manner and they were all Lords Chancellor of England! This sanctuary for elopers and their subsequent marriage was popular with English runaways since under the Scottish law system a marriage could be solemnised by a simple declaration before witnesses.

On the 7th May 1787 Robert Burns crossed the bridge to set foot in England for the first time and to commemorate this event the Cornhill Burns Club in 1926 fixed a bronze plate to the bridge with the inscription "Robert Burns crossed this bridge entering England for the first time 7th May 1787, and kneeling prayed for a blessing on his native land in the words:

"O Scotia! my dear, my native soil!
For whom my warmest wish to Heaven is sent!
Long may thy hardy sons of rustic toil
Be blest with health, and peace and sweet content."

On the outskirts of Coldstream is "The Hirsel", a fine Georgian and Victorian house standing in attractive grounds through which flows the delightful little Leet Water. The grounds are open to the public all year and the visitors' interest is encouraged by a call at the Estate Interpretation Centre. Some one hundred and seventy species of birds have been recorded and there are fine displays of snowdrops, daffodils, azaleas and rhododendrons and a magnificent and diverse array of trees. These include a tulip tree planted in 1742 and a sycamore in the region of four hundred years old. The former is now almost completely hollow but a few flowers are still produced while the sycamore's branches are supported by wire ropes. There is also a large artificial lake, a sanctuary for a wide variety of waterfowl and an embankment to the river which is of interest because it was constructed by French prisoners of the Napoleonic wars and still called the "Maigre".

The seat for many generations of the Earls of Home was in its early days spelt Herisille, meaning "a flock of sheep". Part of the estate at one time belonged to a Cistercian Priory founded by an Earl of Dunbar and March and some time ago a quantity of bones and a stone coffin were unearthed. The bones were believed to be those of members of the Scottish nobility who fell at Flodden and were brought to "The Hirsel" for burial in the consecrated ground of the priory.

The fourteenth and present Earl was Secretary of State for Foreign Affairs in the Conservative administration of Harold Macmillan and succeeded him as Prime Minster in 1963. His son and heir, Lord Dunglass, was christened David Alexander Cospatrick Douglas-Home after Comes Patrick, grandson of King Duncan, from whom the family can trace its descent, and who was murdered by Macbeth. The peerage was created in 1473 and in 1605 the sixth of that line received an Earldom. The ex-prime-minister's brother, William, is the famous playwright.

One of the Earl's ancestors was delegated by James IV to deal with the Earl of Surrey's flanks at Flodden and to hold the ford across the Tweed at Wark. The first operation was carried out very thoroughly but he was unable to accomplish his second instruction which in any case became academic since the Scottish forces, having been decimated in the battle, had no cause to use the ford. The unfortunate Earl and his men were accused of cowardice and desertion in the face of the enemy and when one of the battle survivors, Fletcher of Selkirk, whom we have already encountered, returned to the town he coined the phrase: —

"Up wi' the Souters of Selkirk,
And down wi' the craven Lord Home!"

The fourteenth Earl claims that his family were only finally forgiven and exonerated when the freedom of the burgh was conferred on him in 1963.

"The Hirsel", ancestral home of the Earls of Home.

Cornhill is an agricultural village situated in rich cornlands and with but a single street at the end of which is the Elizabethan hall of the Collingwood family standing on a terraced lawn on a site once occupied by the peel tower of "Cornell" destroyed by the Earl of Fife in 1335, rebuilt and taken by a troop of Scots led by the French General D'Esse in 1549. A mile to the north east near the old ford of Lennel stands the "Castleton Nich" peel tower built in 1121.

On the south side of St Helen's Church is "The Bathing-well Plantation", where a small bath-house once stood on the banks of a little stream. The bath-house was situated above St Helen's Well which was famed for its medicinal properties especially in connection with the treatment of gravel and scurvy. Nearby in Camp Field are the remains of entrenchments, a further reminder of the unhappy history of these parts. In contrast there is a natural formation below the bridge over the Tweed known as the Cornhill Dyke; this is a basalt outcrop stretching some seven miles in a north-easterly direction and is a sharply contrasting geological feature to the predominant limestone of the area.

Cornhill is a great fox hunting centre and the kennels of the North Northumberland foxhounds are situated there, the hunt area being largely of grass and moorland.

A mile or two back on the Cornhill to Kelso road there is the village of Wark where between the river and the road was fought a bitter battle in 1016 in which Uhtred, Earl of Northumberland, was defeated by Malcolm of Scotland and Owain the Bald of Strathclyde. The village is an attractive place built in no particular line or conformity and with the remains of an early twelfth century castle built by Walter d'Espee. Very little of the castle now remains, only fragments of the south-west tower which in its prime would have been about 120 feet high and from which signals could be sent to Norham and Berwick. The castle is referred to in an old manuscript as "the honour of Carham" and was an important border fortress for several centuries. Walter d'Espee was granted the honour of the manor of Carham by Henry I and the Lord of the Manor presides every third year in the school room over the Court-leet, a body of local inhabitants elected to the surveillance of matters affecting the running of the manor.

Between 1136 and 1523 the Scots besieged the castle on no less than eleven occasions, Edward I marched his army into Scotland from it and there Edward II mustered his army in preparation for the Battle of Bannockburn. There also, according to the chronicler, Froissart, the Countess of Salisbury royally entertained Edward III. It was this entertaining that brought about the institution of the oldest surviving British order of chivalry resulting from an incident at a court ball in 1349. During the course of the festivities the Countess dropped her garter which was immediately retrieved by Edward and given back to her. Observing some of his courtiers smiling he remonstrated with them using the memorable words "Honi soit qui mal y pense" — "Evil be to him who evil thinks" and adding "shortly you shall see that garter advanced to so high an honour and renown as to account yourselves happy to wear it". Now the Order of the Garter is in the gift of the Sovereign and awarded to persons who have accorded great and distinguished service to the nation.

The castle was erected at the east end of a ridge of drift gravel running a mile or so in the direction of Carham and known as the Kaim. The ridge is 150 feet wide at the base, 13 feet wide at the top with a height of 60 feet and was caused by glacial action and the currents of an ancient sea.

94

Before leaving the Coldstream area to proceed downstream it is essential that a deviation from the river should be made to visit the scene of one of Scotland's greatest military disasters, Flodden Field and its environs. The site of the battlefield lies in the parish of Branxton just west of the A697 road to Wooler. On the crest of Piper's Hill on Branxton Moor the Berwick Naturalists' Club erected a tall Celtic cross of grey Aberdeen granite standing on a cairn of rough granite blocks. It was unveiled in 1910 by the Kelso poet and essayist, Sir George Douglas, and bears the simple inscription "Flodden 1513. To the brave of both nations."

The battle was fought on the 9th September and though of major proportions for battles of that time it was linked to greater events taking place on the continent of Europe. James IV and his brother-in-law, Henry VIII, had a treaty of perpetual friendship, but Scotland had a still older treaty with France that affected England's mission in Europe which was quite simply to prevent France from conquering Spain and vice versa. Victory for either country over the other would have made the victor master of the continent and drastically reduced England's hopes of continued national independence to a minimum.

On the 13th June Henry crossed to France in consequence of which James decided to take advantage of the weakened English forces at home by invading England at the end of August with a considerable Scottish army, thereby indirectly going to the aid of his French ally. He also had a personal axe to grind in that he was dissatisfied with the dowry he received with his bride, Margaret Tudor, Henry VIII's sister. James' first objective was either to capture or neutralise the border fortresses, thus securing his flanks and rear, and this he accomplished without too much difficulty, finally occupying what appeared to be an impregnable entrenched position on Flodden Hill. The English forces were under the command of the Earl of Surrey who advanced from his base at Alnwick, keeping the Till on his left flank. His objective was to outflank the Scottish forces which he achieved either by defective information reaching James about the disposition of the English forces or by the King's supineness or a combination of both. Whatever the reason Surrey was able to ford the Till with part of his force at Twizel Mill, the remainder crossing at Sandyford, both groups uniting behind Branxton Marsh. James threw away what strategic advantage he had by descending the hill to accept battle.

The skill of the English archers was too much for the Scots and the havoc they wreaked was followed by complete decimation accomplished by bill and battleaxe. The wielders of these weapons mowed down those of the enemy the archers had left, crushing both flanks in turn and then the centre where James himself, surrounded by the flower of his nobility, was killed along with his natural son, an archbishop, a bishop, two abbots, twelve earls, fourteen lords and many knights and gentlemen. There was hardly a noble family in

Scotland that did not mourn a father, son or brother at the end of that terrible day when the Earls of Argyle, Athol, Bothwell, Caithness, Cassilis, Crawford, Errol, Glencairn, Lennox, Montrose, Morton and Rothes all lay dead on the battlefield. Ten thousand Scots and five thousand English died with them. The body of James was taken to St Paul's Church, Branxton, where it rested the night after the battle; the following day it was taken to Berwick and finally to its last resting place at Sheen in Surrey. A monument near Branxton Church marks the spot where James fell.

The Flodden Memorial on Piper's Hill, Branxton Moor.

Coinciding with Coldstream's Civic Week in August a young man is selected by the townspeople to ride at the head of a cavalcade of horsemen up to a hundred strong to a wreath-laying ceremony at the memorial cross. The party then climbs to the summit of Branxton Hill where a service is held and an address given by some local notability. The proceedings conclude with the pipes playing "Flowers o' the Forest" for it was Flodden that provided Jane Elliott with the inspiration to write the lament which tears at the heart. Scott also wrote a famous lament in "Marmion" for the Scottish nobility who fell in battle: —

96

"Their King, their Lords, their mightiest low,
They melted from the field as snow,
When streams are swoln and south winds blow,
Dissolves in silent dew.
Tweed's echoes hears a ceaseless plash,
While many a broken band
Disorder'd, through her current dash,
To gain the Scottish land,
To Town and tower, to down and dale,
To tell red Flodden's dismal tale,
And raise the universal wail.
Tradition, legend, tune and song,
Shall many an age that wail prolong;
Still from the sire the son shall hear
Of the stern strife and carnage drear;
Of Flodden's fatal field,
Where shiver'd was fair Scotland's spear,
And broken was her shield!"

The tiny village of Branxton is probably unknown to most people and yet it has an important place in Anglo-Scottish history even though the battle took its name from Flodden Hill, about two miles away. Branxton Moor is now good agricultural land and on a clear day there is a splendid view away into Scotland to the romantic Eildon Hills and the remains of the old Forest of Selkirk, deep blue in the distance. Now all is quiet and peaceful, the birds sing and the little farming community goes about its daily tasks undisturbed, a far cry from the sad and terrible events of that September day so long ago.

Overlooking Flodden is the interesting modern mansion known as "Pallinsburn House". Amongst its treasures is the "Adoration of the Shepherds" by Bassano and the flag under which the Grenadier Guards fought at Waterloo. Just below the house is a lake named the "Kaim Bog" in which Paulinus is said to have baptised thousands of converts and which is an important breeding area of black-headed gulls. Hereabouts is a noted geological feature, a detrital ridge called the "kaim", mainly comprising rolled shingle from a series of Silurian rocks of greywacke and, like the similar feature at Wark, is presumed to have been formed by glacial and sea action many aeons ago. A mile to the west of the "Kaim Bog" stands a 7 feet high prehistoric limestone monolith called "The King's Stone" from a mistaken belief that it was erected by Surrey to commemorate his victory at Flodden. In ancient times it probably served the purpose of a border gathering stone.

CHAPTER ELEVEN

Coldstream to Berwick

SOON after leaving Coldstream the Tweed is joined at Tillworth Park by its only all English tributary of any importance. The Till starts life as the Breamish (bright water) on Scotsmans Knowe high in the Cheviots and is soon augmented by the Glen into which run the peaty waters of the College Burn at Kirknewton. Collectively these become the Till at Bewick Mill. All this area is wild and beautiful in summer but cruel and dangerous when the winter blizzards and storms are blowing in all their fury. The Cheviots are in the main grass-covered, which suits the hardy indigenous sheep, but bracken and heather take over towards the summits which are boggy and snow covered for a good part of the year.

Though some way south of the Tweed and slightly away from the Till it is nevertheless appropriate to mention Lilburn Tower because of its family connections with Wark Castle. The tower stands south-east of Wooler just eastwards of the A697 to Newcastle-upon-Tyne. It has been the home of the Collingwood family since 1793 though the famous admiral was born in 1750 at Newcastle where Millburn House now stands. Cuthbert Collingwood was one of the gallant officers who helped to gain the victories that Nelson planned and he took part in most of the naval battles of the Napoleonic wars and was second in command at Trafalgar, after which he was awarded a peerage. He died in 1810 and lies at rest near Nelson in St Paul's Cathedral.

About half way on the main road between Coldstream and Wooler is the village of Millfield where Josephine Butler was born in Millfield House. She was a great reformer and worked hard to overcome the many social evils of the nineteenth century. She was buried in the churchyard of Kirknewton where the church has a carving of the Virgin Mary and the Wise Men, curious in that the Magi are depicted wearing kilts! Downstream from Kirknewton is Coupland Castle, one of the few fortified castles built after the Union.

Opposite Branxton and Flodden, but separated from them by the Coldstream to Wooler road, is the beautiful village of Ford dominated by the eighteenth century castle, one time seat of the Marchioness of Waterford, a bridesmaid of Queen Victoria, and now the property of Lord Joicey. The village is a little gem with its delightful cottages and gardens situated on a gentle slope between the highway and the castle gates with a broad carriage-drive passing through it which is edged with trimly cut grass-covered banks.

The castle, former seat of Lord Joicey and now an educational centre, was built between 1761 and 1764 by Sir John Hussay Delaval and stands in fine grounds on a hill overlooking the Till and the village with widespread views towards the Cheviots, the Flodden battlefield and Wooler. Delaval's castle was based on the tower of a fortress built in 1287 by Odenel de Forde who married the daughter of Sir William Heron. Sir William must have been on good terms with Edward III because not only was he High Sheriff of Northumberland for eleven years but also warden of all the forests north of the Trent and captain of the castles at Bamburgh, Pickering and Scarborough. The castle suffered like so many others in the Borders and was taken successively by the Earls of Fife, March and Douglas before being demolished in 1385. Although it was partially rebuilt it was again severely damaged in 1549 by the Frenchman, Sieur D'Esse. It is reputed to be the possessor of a ghost, that of James IV who can sometimes be heard putting on his armour in the king's chamber!

The interesting church of St Michael was restored in 1853 and here are buried Lord Fitzclarence and his daughter, Augusta Georgina, who survived her father only a few months. His Lordship was one of ten offspring of the association William IV had with Mrs Jordan.

In the school of this little village there is something which is almost without doubt unique and strangely moving. The walls are graced by a series of nine watercolours executed by the Marchioness of Waterford (1818-91) including the blessing of little children by Christ which forms the subject of a fresco on one of the end walls, the faces depicted being those of the village children of her time. Elsewhere on the walls are ornamental medallions containing representations of themes relevant to the main subject of each incident taken from the Old Testament.

Subject	*Medallion*
1. Cain and Abel	Adam and Eve, apple in flower and fruit
2. Abraham and Isaac	The angel and the ram with the brambles of the thicket
3. Jacob and Esau	Isaac and Rebecca with oak leaves
4. Joseph and his Brethren	The Baker and Butler with sheaves of corn
5. Moses in the bulrushes	Moses and Aaron with bulrushes
6. Samuel given to the Lord	Eli and the child Samuel with the first fruits of corn, grapes and olives
7. David the Shepherd	Saul and David with vine
8. Josiah made king at eight years of age	Huldah and Hilkiah and the cutting down of the groves
9. The three children	Daniel and the hand writing on the wall with tree in life and death

Included in the Visitors' Book are the signatures of W. E. Gladstone, Sir Edwin Landseer, Earl Grey, Lord Stratford de Redcliffe, the Earl of Shrewsbury and Talbot, Earl Cowper, Earl Brownlow, Earl of Gainsborough, Earl of Home, Duke of Buccleuch and Queensberry, Princess Christian of

Schleswig-Holstein, the Duke of St Albans, the Dean of Westminster and Lady Augusta Stanley, Lord Redesdale, Earl Stirling Maxwell, Lord Armstrong, Lord Houghton, Earl of Warwick, Professor Huxley, Earl of Crawford and Balcarres, Sidney Herbert, Professor Fairbairn, Sir Charles Trevelyan, the Duke of Teck, Princess Mary of Teck and those of many other persons of distinction.

Just down the road from Ford is Etal, which probably in the recent past would have rivalled its neighbour in a competition for the prettiest village. Formerly the low grey-walled cottages with overhanging eaves, rounded doors and windows and typical cottage gardens had thatched roofs, but alas all except two or three of these have been replaced by tile and slate and most of the walls are now whitewashed. Even the *Black Bull* had a thatched roof but now the whole building has been demolished and the village regrettably is not as charming as it used to be.

The end of the road for King Salmon.

Scottish Tourist Board

The Church of the Blessed Virgin Mary was built and endowed in 1850 by the Rt. Hon. Lady Fitzclarence in memory of her husband and only child who, as we have seen, are buried in Ford Church. Etal Church is situated in the grounds of the Manor which was built in 1748 by Sir William Carr and enlarged in 1767; it is the residence of Lord Joicey.

At the other end of the village are the ruins of the Castle, once the stronghold of Sir Robert de Manners, an ancestor of the Duke of Rutland, who was licensed by Edward III to crenellate his mansion in 1341. The keep and gate-house still remain and in front of the latter once stood two guns salvaged from the *Royal George* which sank near Spithead with the loss of over three hundred lives on the 29th August 1782. Near the castle, which was destroyed by James IV prior to his defeat and death at Flodden, can be seen the foundations of a bridge across the Till over which the captured Scottish artillery was transported on the day after the battle.

The Till is particularly beautiful as it flows past Etal between thickly wooded banks and then on past a high escarpment known as "Big Nichol" which is between Tiptoe Mill and Tiptoe Throat, the curious name given to the stretch of water at this point. Just below Etal Mill lie the remains of St Mary's Chantry founded in 1346 by the builder of the castle, Sir Robert de Manners, and adjoining which is St Mary's Well. When the Chantry site was excavated a human skull was exposed and found to contain a wren's nest.

The quaintly named village of Duddo stands on a freestone escarpment close to a ruinous peel tower which once belonged to the Lords of Tillmouth and was destroyed by the Scots as part of their softening-up procedure before Flodden. Duddo gets its name from "dod" meaning a round-topped hill and "hoe" meaning a height and certainly the village has sufficient height above the surrounding Merse for it to have extensive views of the Cheviot, Eildon and Lammermuir Hills. On nearby Grindon Rig is the site of an ancient British burial ground from which several funerary urns have been excavated. Encircling this spot are the Duddo stones, five large monoliths of deeply furrowed red freestone between five and ten feet high forming part of a circle forty feet in circumference. Opposite the stones on the other side of the village is Watchlow Hill from which Surrey and his officers watched the progress of the Battle of Flodden.

Having digressed to explore the beauties of the Till and its interesting and pretty villages it is time to rejoin the Tweed and this is accomplished close by the eighteenth century Twizel Castle standing in an angle formed by the two rivers; the ruin looks older than it is because the architecture is decidedly Norman in style. Here it was that the fate of the Scottish army at Flodden was sealed when James IV negligently allowed the English forces to ford the Till without opposition.

The river is crossed by the picturesque Twizel Bridge which is the lowest over the Till, with a stone single arch spanning 90 feet, and of which the chronicler, John Leland, referred "of stone one bow, but greate and stronge." After flowing by the now disused railway line the Till meets the Tweed opposite an island which has the distinction of being half in England and half in Scotland. Near here is a somewhat undistinguished stone building with gable walls and window apertures but without a roof. Undistinguished perhaps but it has achieved immortality in verse since this was the chapel to which the heroine of "Marmion" fled after Flodden and which inspired Scott's memorable words: —

> " 'Oh! lady!' cried the monk, 'away'
> And placed her on her steed,
> And led her to the chapel fair
> Of Tillmouth upon Tweed.
> There all the night they spent in prayer,
> And at the dawn of morning, there
> She met her kinsman, Lord Fitz-Clare."

A man of many parts lies in the churchyard. Percival Stockdale was born in 1736 at Branxton, the only son of the vicar. After attending Alnwick and Berwick Grammar Schools he became a poetry lover and classical scholar, joined the army and was one of Admiral John Byng's men sent on the abortive attempt to relieve Port St Philip on the island of Minorca, which was being blockaded by the French in 1757. Byng's failure was to cost him his life because on his return to England he was court martialled on a charge of cowardice and sentenced to be shot on the deck of his own ship. Stockdale was happily more fortunate than the ill-fated admiral, but he was obliged to leave the army due to ill-health in 1757. He had reached Durham on his way home when he encountered the Archdeacon of Northumberland who inspired, persuaded or cajoled him into taking holy orders. This sudden transformation from the laity to the clergy resulted in a curacy in London where he became friendly with Oliver Goldsmith and Dr Samuel Johnson; later he became vicar of Lesbury, where he died, and Long Houghton. He was a prolific writer but most of his work has sunk into oblivion except for a book published in 1802 at Alnwick, entitled *Memoirs and Remonstrances against Inhumanity to Animals, particularly against the Savage Practice of Bull-Baiting.* In spite of its verbose title it probably created something of a sensation at a time when, regrettably, cruelty to animals was generally accepted as commonplace and not worthy of concern. The laudable Percival could never know that he was sowing a seed that as the years went by would produce ever more fruit.

Just below the confluence is Ladykirk which owes its name to a vow made by James IV, who was in danger of drowning when fording the river. The king declared that if he survived the crossing he would build a church in honour of the Virgin and he was as good as his word, not only in building the church but giving its name to the village which grew around it. Edward I is also connected with this locality since it was at nearby Upsettlington that he obtained promises of vassalship from candidates for the Scottish throne.

On the English bank opposite Ladykirk is the salmon village of Norham in whose ancient and beautiful church the daughter of Lord Home was married in the 1960's. It is built on the site of a chapel founded in 830 where St Ceowulf, King of Northumbria, was buried and to whom the Venerable Bede dedicated his famous history. An interesting feature of the present church is that cross fragments, discovered when the foundations were being prepared and dating from the time of the original building, have been set up in the form of a pillar inside the massive tower. The body of Dr William Stephen Gilly lies in the church, where he became vicar in 1831. He is remembered for the interest he aroused in the social conditions of the peasantry of the Borders and Northern Italy. Before dying in 1855 he had published *A Narrative of an Excursion to the Mountains of Piedmont* and *Research Among the Vaudois or Waldenses*. Public sympathy and interest were aroused by these books on the oppressed Vaudois and a subscription list was headed by William IV and the Bishop of Durham. Nearer home he was incensed by the attitudes of landowners of the Borders to the miserable conditions in which they were prepared to allow their tenants to live; he exposed this deplorable state of affairs in his *Peasantry of the Border; an appeal on their behalf.*

Lovers of Sir Walter Scott's works will be familiar with Norham Castle for it was this magnificent edifice that Sir William Marmion chose to prove his love by risking his life: —

"Day set on Norham's castle steep
And Tweed's fair river, broad and deep
And Cheviot's mountain lone:
The battled tower, the donjon keep
The loop-holed walls where captives weep
In yellow lustre shone."

The original building was a timber structure erected in 1121 by Bishop Ranulph Flambard as the main border stronghold of the Bishops of Durham. It was twice taken by the Scots during incursions culminating in the Battle of the Standard which took place in 1138 near Northallerton in North Yorkshire. The battle received its name from the circumstance that a sacred standard, composed of the banners of Saints Peter, John and Wilfred, was created on the battlefield. David I, who had invaded the north of England on behalf of his niece, Matilda, daughter of Henry I who had died that year, was defeated by forces raised by Thurston, Archbishop of York. Henry II reconquered Northumberland and then in 1160 timber gave way to stone when the keep, the broken fragment of which is all that remains, was erected by Bishop Hugh of Puiset or Pudsey. The stone building did not remain long in the possession of the bishops because it was confiscated by King John who received there homage from William the Lion in 1209. In an effort to retrieve the Castle for Scotland Alexander II laid siege to it for three months in 1215 but to no avail.

Edward I in 1291 listened to the pleas of thirteen claimants to the Scottish throne and awarded the honour to John Balliol whose parents had founded Balliol College, Oxford. The following year Edward received John's homage at Newcastle. The rival factions had agreed that Edward should be an impartial arbiter and Edward accepted provided the successful candidate would be prepared to pay homage to him for the whole of Scotland. Another unsuccessful siege lasted nearly a year in 1318 when Robert Bruce attempted to overcome the garrison under the command of Sir Thomas Grey and he was equally unsuccessful a year later; this says much for the tenacity and courage of the besieged and the quality and solidity of the stronghold. In both sieges Bruce had the audacity to use the church as his headquarters. The strength of the fortress was again put to the test in 1497 when Mons Meg, the great cannon forged in Flanders and brought to Scotland about 1450 and now gracing the walls of Edinburgh Castle, was brought from there to assist in an attempt to overcome the defences but even this proved inadequate to bring about the Castle's downfall. What proved too tough a proposition for Mons Meg was not so obstinate when James IV laid siege to the Castle in 1513 on his way to disaster and death at Flodden because he was able to affect its capture after inflicting considerable damage to the structure with heavy artillery.

Today the Castle is a delight to visit surrounded as it is by fine beech trees and lawns, with the west gate, Marmion's Gate, facing the road leading down to the village. Ruinous though it is the original spaciousness of its former glory can be easily traced, reflecting its long and turbulent history high above the steep river bank overlooking the ancient ford.

Apart from the Castle's romantic connection with Walter Scott's writings it also has a real life romantic association because in 1549 John Knox, the turbulent priest, met Margaret Bowes, daughter of the governor, and she eventually became his wife. Even such a firebrand anti-papist as John occasionally relaxed from his intolerant, vitriolic outbursts and gave over himself to the more pleasant affairs of the heart. Ten years later George Carleton was born; he was the son of the then governor and, after becoming Bishop of Chichester, wrote the biography of his first teacher, Bernard Gilpin, the Apostle of the North.

The village of Norham is a pleasant little place of grey cottages lining a long main street with a green and market cross which has a weather vane in the form of a fish, emblematic of the connection the village has with the salmon fishing industry. Each year at midnight on the 13th February a unique ceremony is performed by the vicar of Norham when he blesses the fishermen and their nets from a coble in the river at the commencement of the new fishing season. The service is conducted by lantern light and opens with the well known passage of the miraculous draught of fishes from St John's Gospel. This is followed by a prayer, the singing of the doxology — "Praise God from Whom all blessings flow" — and an address by the vicar. At the conclusion of the service the nets are cast into the water and the first catch accomplished.

The Tweed is now rapidly approaching the sea and Horncliffe, six miles from the mouth, is the limit of the tidal reach and navigability. The village stands on a red cliff above the river and the surrounding area, including Horncliffe Dene with its waterfall, is a great favourite of fishermen and botanist. In 1639 the Royalist army camped on land in the bend of the river where there is a ford which is one of the lowest in the whole length of the Tweed. The Commonwealth army encamped nearby after crossing the ford and at the lower end of the village there used to be a pair of thatched cottages which were reputed to have sheltered Cromwell and some of his officers.

The Union Bridge at Horncliffe.

Small though it is Horncliffe can boast of the first big suspension bridge in the United Kingdom. The Union Bridge, built in 1820, is 432 feet long between the suspension points, 18 feet wide and 69 feet above water level. On the south side the chains start from a massive abutment built into the red cliff and cross to a stone arch on the north bank which is an impressive entry into Scotland. The designer of the bridge was a Royal Naval Captain, Sir Samuel Brown, who invented a revolutionary type of link for chain cables which enabled bigger suspension bridges to be erected in the future. Brown went on to design a chain pier at Brighton and his principle was adopted by Thomas Telford in the construction of the Menai Bridge.

Half-way between Horncliffe and Berwick, the Tweed receives its last tributary, Whiteadder Water flowing in from the north. Just west of the confluence is the village of Paxton where the song "Robin Adair" originated, and where, overlooking the river, "Paxton House" is situated, another fine example of Adam's architecture and the home of the Milne-Home family. Close by is the partially ruined Hutton Castle which, until a few years ago, housed a large part of Sir William Burrell's famous art collection which now belongs to the city of Glasgow. To the east the border strikes due north for two miles to Mordington where Robert the Bruce's chaplain and secretary was vicar. Bernard de Linton later became Abbot of Arbroath and Chancellor of Scotland and compiled The Declaration of Independence of 1320. Higher up the Whiteadder at its junction with the Blackadder ("adder" being a corruption of water) in Chirnside churchyard is the grave of James Clark, world motor racing champion in 1962 and 1965, who was killed in 1968 on the track at Hockenheim near Frankfurt-on-Main. Jim was born in Fifeshire in 1942 but became a Chirnsider at the age of six when his farming parents moved to the village. After leaving Loretto at sixteen he joined his father on the farm but soon took to motor racing, winning his first event at Aberdeen a year later. Mechanical contrivances had always fascinated him and he was a "natural" to racing. There is a clock memorial to him made from Welsh blue sandstone surmounted by an iron racing car skeleton in the village. Jim was an honorary burgess of Duns where there is a James Clark memorial room in the council building displaying a large number of his trophies.

Chirnside churchyard was the scene of an extraordinary incident in the late seventeenth century with the burial of Margaret Erskine, the wife of the minister. On their marriage Henry had given his bride a ring, a cluster of five diamonds, which she greatly prized and requested should remain on her finger at her funeral. When the mourners had left the graveside the sexton, John Carr, opened the coffin and tried to remove the ring, whereupon Margaret scrambled out of the grave, for she had been in a trance, and returned home to her astonished but delighted husband saying, when she reached the house, "Let me in, let me in, I'm fair clemmed wi' the cauld". She and Henry lived happily for many years, raising two sons in the process to add to the five children she had borne before her "death". It is not recorded what the reactions of the sexton were to what must have been something of a nerve-racking experience, but it is doubtful if he ever again attempted to repeat coffin opening for the purposes of theft.

The tithe barn at Foulden.

The neighbouring village of Edrom was also the venue early in the nineteenth century of a macabre event in the Burke and Hare tradition, these two infamous gentlemen not being the only ones involved in the body snatching business, which provided one had the stomach for it, could be quite a profitable venture. Late one evening a couple of men were returning home when they overtook a coach with three occupants, one of whom appeared to be lifeless. Much intrigued and decidedly suspicious, for they were well aware that grave robbing was a common practice, the men stopped the coach from which the robbers, for robbers they were, disappeared into the night with considerable alacrity. The corpse proved to be that of a man buried a few days earlier at Edrom. The coach was taken to Duns where it was smashed to pieces and burned by an angry mob and such was the disturbance that the Riot Act had to be read.

Edrom possesses a house built in the side of a rock with one room up and one down. Now very dilapidated it was inhabited until well into the present century even though it possessed no light, sanitation or water.

Between Edrom and the neighbouring village of Preston there is a most unusual bridge, known as the Cuddy Brig, beneath which is a small but soundly built room, with an aperture for sanitation purposes over the burn. Built in 1771, its original purpose was probably the overnight accommodation of prisoners on their way to Greenlaw to stand trial. Eventually it became a haven for vagrants and finally a stable.

This area seems to have gathered around it more than its share of improbable happenings and a third to add to the two previous ones concerns the erection of a bridge over Whiteadder Water near its junction with the Billy Burn. Now this bridge building had been made possible by a legacy left for the purpose by a well-known and thrifty local packman who had stipulated the exact position he had wished it to be sited. The bridge was, however, built in a different spot and was twice swept away by floods before, in 1782, being placed in the exact situation at Billyburnfoot specified by the benefactor; no more was it washed away and it is still standing. The packman's voice was heard by the workmen each time they completed the abortive erections, uttering a posthumous curse: —

"Hyndhaugh brig, and Hyndhaugh brae,
Hyndhaugh brig shall slide away;
Hyndhaugh brig shall never stand
For breaking o' the dead's command,
But left it to Billy-Burn fit,
And there it will stand for ages yet,
And there it will stand as firm's the Bass
Till owre a thousand years shall pass."

Foulden lies to the east of Chirnside and possesses a fine two-storeyed tithe barn with crow-stepped gables and external staircase. The village was the place where in 1587 Queen Elizabeth's Commissioners met to vindicate the execution of Mary, Queen of Scots.

In 1803 Joseph Paxton was born in Duns, later moving to London and becoming a gardener at Chiswick where his botanical knowledge so impressed the Duke of Devonshire that he made him Chatsworth gardens' manager. It was here that Joseph was given the opportunity and encouragement to design horticultural buildings of glass and iron, these being the forerunner of his plans for Crystal Palace which housed the Great Exhibition of 1851. He was responsible for the layouts of many famous gardens with their fountains and terraces, became Member of Parliament for Coventry and received a knighthood in 1854. Duns was also the birthplace in 1266 of the famous philosopher and theologian, John Duns Scotus, who spent a good part of his forty-two years denouncing the teaching of Thomas Aquinas. A bronze statue was erected in 1966 by the Franciscan Order of the Roman Catholic church marking the seven hundredth anniversary of his birth, the site of which near the castle is marked by a cairn.

It has fallen to poor Duns Scotus to be remembered in our language by the word "dunce" which came into use during the Commonwealth period nearly two and a half centuries after his death. Humanists had no use for Dun's philosophy and "dunce" was the derogatory word coined by Cromwell's Puritans to express their displeasure—even disgust—of his views.

Duns, the word means a "hill defence", represented by 714 feet high Duns Law, was the county town of Berwickshire from 1903-75 when it lost its status with local government reorganisation, but it has an ancient lineage, having been made a royal burgh in 1489 by James IV. It is now a thriving market town and something of an old-world atmosphere still remains in the Market Square. The Castle Nature Reserve is an interesting woodland area with many species of animal, bird and plant life, including wildfowl on the lake. In 1639 General Alexander Leslie with two thousand Covenanters stationed themselves on the Law to oppose the army of Charles I advancing to enforce Episcopalianism on the country. The Covenanters took an oath — "For Christ's Crown and Covenant" — and planted their standard on a large block of red sandstone known today as the Covenanters' Stone.

Just outside the town stands Scotland's finest Edwardian mansion, Manderston House, set in grounds which include a lake and a fine cricket field. The architect was John Kinross, who previously had restored Falkland Palace for the third Marquis of Bute: his work on the Manderston outbuildings has made them the finest group of modern recreative Scots architecture in existence. There is a tea-room and a folly dairy, folly because it is made of marble, in the border tower, but in spite of its mundane usage its restoration displays a knowledge and understanding of historic buildings that would be difficult to surpass. Added interest is that septs and ornamentation from the old quadrangle of Glasgow University, demolished last century, have been incorporated in the restoration.

For the last three miles of its course the Tweed becomes an English river, having for the previous nineteen miles from Carham been the boundary between the two countries, the border being in the centre of the river. So, though predominantly a Scottish river, England does at least share it for part of its course and possesses it exclusively for an even smaller part. All the way from Kelso the river has flowed across the Merse, an area of wide open spaces and great skyscapes, an area of 130,000 acres unspoiled by industry and, as previously mentioned, largely given over to rich farmland with only two centres of population of any size, the burgs of Coldstream and Duns.

ON THIS STONE ACCORDING
TO UNBROKEN TRADITION WAS
RAISED THE STANDARD OF THE
COVENANTERS WHEN IN 1639
THEIR ARMY UNDER GENERAL SIR
ALEX LESLIE ASSEMBLED
ON DUNS LAW

The Covenanters' Stone where the oath "For Christ's Crown and Covenant" was taken.

CHAPTER TWELVE

Berwick on Tweed

A S THE river approaches the sea it has, in the last few miles, to pass the most interesting and historic town of its whole course. Berwick on Tweed is the most northerly town in England and the only English town on the "wrong" side of the river, situated as it is on the north bank. It has a long and chequered history characterised by the cruel and barbarous feuds and wars that raged throughout the Middle Ages between the English and the Scots and which extended to a greater or lesser degree down to the eighteenth century. A visitor to the town can still see ample evidence of the hostility that for centuries plagued and bedevilled the two nations and more especially the inhabitants of the areas immediately north and south of the border.

The geographical situation of the town has created a curious and anomalous situation in that it is politically part of Northumberland and yet also a Scottish royal burgh. It was once independent of both England and Scotland and styled "The County of the Borough and Town of Berwick-on-Tweed" and as such was specially mentioned in Acts of Parliament until 1746. This state of affairs prevailed until the Reform Act of 1885.

It is still in many ways in a state of limbo in that it is the Headquarters of a Scottish regiment, the Queen's Own Borderers, and its Association Football team plays in the Scottish League.

Berwick is a compact and picturesque little town with a population of about twelve thousand and is undoubtedly one of the best examples of a fortified town in the whole of the British Isles. It was probably founded by the Saxons soon after they had gained a foothold on English soil and the name equally probably derives from Bere or Bar Wic — a corn or grain farm or port — which signifies the commercial aspect of its foundation and which it has maintained down the ages to the present day. However, there is now little maritime trade left though grain, timber and fertiliser are still imported and barley exported. The decline stems from the growth of the great industrial conurbation of Tyneside some sixty miles to the south and the fact that Berwick itself has no industrial hinterland to support it as a port. It still flourishes as a market town, being the centre of a considerable agricultural area. It has a chartered right to hold two weekly markets on Wednesdays and Saturdays and there is also a cattle and sheep market and a fair lasting for eight days commencing on Trinity Sunday.

Looking north across the river from Tweedmouth to Berwick on Tweed.

The earliest history of Berwick is lost in the mists of time but it is known that roving bands of Picts and Scots under Donald and Gregory the Great plundered the town. Malcolm II took Lothian from Northumbria in 1018 at the battle of Carham, thereby establishing the Tweed as the boundary between England and Scotland. Duncan, who succeeded Malcolm as King of the Scots, fitted out eleven ships in the port to oppose Macbeth and the town was sacked by mercenaries of William the Conqueror. The first authentic reference to Berwick is a charter granted by King Edgar to the See of Durham by which it received the town, its churches and possessions. In succeeding reigns it became Scotland's chief port and was created one of four royal burghs — the others being Edinburgh, Roxburgh and Stirling — by David I and thus achieved the dubious distinction of becoming the focal point between the rival kingdoms. The town and its surroundings was the scene of constant strife for nearly three hundred and fifty years and changed hands thirteen times between 1147 and 1482 when it finally passed to the English crown.

In 1147 William the Lion was captured at Alnwick and in order to obtain his freedom was forced to cede the town to Henry II; however Scotland regained the town in 1189 by the simple expedient of providing a financial contribution to Richard I's crusading zeal. As most of Richard's reign was occupied in warring in foreign parts, Berwick for a time was left in peace but

112

shortly after Richard's death, his brother, John, razed it to the ground. In 1214 he was returning from a foray into Scotland and lodged in the town for a night on his way south. By way of thanks for the night's refreshment and entertainment he personally set fire to the house that had given him shelter and this was the signal for his men to put a light to the rest of the town.

Rebuilding soon commenced and by the time Alexander III came to the throne in 1247 the town was about to commence a period of prosperity which was outstanding and unsurpassed anywhere else in the land outside the capital. This period coincided with Alexander's reign and when he died in 1286 the customs dues for that year amounted to £2,190, largely in respect of hides and wool, and accounted for about one quarter of the dues of the whole country. Such was the prosperity that according to the chronicler, Lanercost, it was "a city so populous and of such trade that it might justly be called another Alexandria, whose riches were the sea and the water its walls." It was said that the town "took rank with Ghent and Rotterdam and was almost a rival of London."

We have already seen that Edward I selected John Balliol to sit on the Scottish throne from the claimants assembled at Norham in 1291. One of them was Robert Bruce, one would think an obvious choice, but no doubt discarded because the king presumed that Balliol would be more pliable and sycophantic than the firebrand, Bruce: in any case Balliol was a stronger claimant than Bruce. Be that as it may it was not long before Edward had cause to regret his choice because five years later Balliol rebelled. Edward's vengeance was swift and terrible, the town being sacked yet again and seven thousand men, women and children put to death. Many Flemish merchants perished when their warehouse, known as the Red Hall, was destroyed with them inside. The town was resettled with English traders but only a year later was captured by William Wallace. This time the Scots' occupation was short lived and Wallace was executed in London in 1305 and part of his body affixed to the town bridge as a warning to any who might be considering further rebellion. The year after Wallace's death, Isabel, the Countess of Buchan, sister of the Earl of Fife, was imprisoned in Berwick Castle for committing the same offence for which Mary Bruce was caged at Roxburgh. She was publicly exposed in an open-wire cage for four years to the derision and invective of the townsfolk and the vagaries of the weather and of the changing seasons. So goes the story, but it is clear from Edward's instructions that such a cage was a device for solitary confinement within a turret.

In 1328 Edward III's sister, Joanna, married Bruce's son, David, as part of treaty terms agreed in an endeavour to patch up some sort of a peace between the two countries. Child marriages were not uncommon in the middle ages and were usually ploys adopted for political, strategic and economic purposes but this one was more absurd than most since David was only four years old and Joanna three years older. A year later David succeeded to the throne and four years after that the marriage purposes were in ruins when the Scots recaptured the town in 1333. Edward, like his predecessor, exacted terrible revenge; he led an army northwards and based it on Halidon Hill, two miles to the north west of Berwick and separated from the town by marshy ground. The Scottish defenders were led by the Regent, Archibald Douglas, and were trapped in the morass as they advanced towards the hill, thus falling easy prey to the English archers and men-at-arms.

The battle is now commemorated by a tall stone monument at the roadside on the hill, from where one can not only ponder and regret the carnage of so long ago but also enjoy the glorious panoramic view of the town below and the coastline from Eyemouth Point in the north to the Farne Islands in the south. Inland are the Eildon Hills above "Abbotsford" whilst close by are some cottages beside the site of Lamberton toll house, which at one time was the Gretna Green of the east coast. Just north of this site is the lion and unicorn monument marking the railway border crossing.

In 1603 James VI of Scotland passed through the town on his way to be crowned James I of England in London and from that time Berwick ceased to be of contention by either country.

Berwick has the unique distinction of having been the headquarters of the only British Army general ever to bring news of his own defeat back to his base. After the Jacobite victory in 1745 at Prestonpans, General John Cope galloped via Lauder and Coldstream to Berwick with the unhappy tidings.

Wherever one wanders in Berwick it is virtually impossible to keep away from reminders of its past, some remote, other comparatively modern. Approaching from the south, the red-roofed grey stone houses can be seen high on the far bank of the Tweed but the most immediate aspects that invite inspection are the three bridges spanning the river. The one furthest upstream is the Royal Border Bridge which carries the main east coast railway between England and Scotland. It was designed by Robert Stephenson, son of George, the inventor of the steam locomotive; building began on the 15th May 1847 and the three years' work cost £253,000. It comprises 28 stone-cased semi-circular arches, is 2,160 feet long and 126 feet at its greatest height above the water surface. It was opened on 29th August 1850 by Queen Victoria accompanied by Prince Albert, who much to the disgust of the inhabitants of the town stopped in the royal train for only ten minutes. Most of them did not even obtain a glimpse of their monarch although much time and trouble had been put into the arrangements for the royal visit.

The middle one of the bridges is the Royal Tweed Bridge opened in 1928 by the Prince of Wales, later Edward VIII and Duke of Windsor. It carries the A1 highway between the two countries, still known to an older generation by its more romantic name of Great North Road. The bridge has four arches

114

of reinforced concrete, the northern span being 361 feet long and the longest concrete span in the country. During construction a peat bed was discovered at foundation level of one of the piers and 186 concrete piles, each 36 feet long and weighing two tons, were used to provide a solid bed.

The Royal Border Bridge, Berwick on Tweed carrying the main east coast rail route across the river.

The Old Bridge, also known as the James VI Bridge, was built between 1611 and 1624 by James Barrell, King's Surveyor at Berwick. It is 1,164 feet long and 17 feet wide with 15 arches, is made of red sandstone and has a small bay at each side above the piers as a refuge for pedestrians. Prior to 1928 it carried the Great North Road across the swirling tidal waters and though still used by motor traffic has given way in importance to its more imposing and modern neighbour. The timber foundations of the original bridge, destroyed in 1199 by a disastrous flood and afterwards rebuilt by William the Lion, are said to be visible about 80 yards upstream.

The Royal Border Bridge has in it stones from the castle, the station occupying most of the castle site, the down platform having been constructed over the part once occupied by the great hall. One cannot help regretting the folly of Robert Stephenson and his contemporaries in allowing the castle to be demolished to make space for the railway. One feels sure that such a thing could not happen nowadays when an alternative route would have been adopted in order to preserve such an important relic of the past and an integral part of the town's history.

The little that now remains of the castle comprises two or three towers on the hill top and the line of curtain walling, known as the White wall, which descends the hill side from the railway to the river.

On entering the town it is immediately apparent that it is bisected in roughly both north-south and east-west directions; one way by Wallace Green, Church Street, Hide Hill and Sandgate and the other way by the Wool Market, Marygate and Castlegate. For a town of such age as Berwick it is remarkable that it possesses so few historic buildings, though this at least can be partly explained by its long and turbulent history with its alternate sackings and destructions and rebuildings. For instance, nothing remains of the ancient churches of St Lawrence, St Mary and St Nicholas or the hospitals belonging to the Black, Grey, Red and White Friars. In 1548 John Knox is said to have preached in St Mary's Church though with what effect on the congregation is not known. One notable survivor of the past, however, is Holy Trinity Church built in the years 1648-53 by John Young, a master of the Masons' Company. It possesses a fine Elizabethan panelled oak pulpit, a relic of an earlier church, and a reredos designed by Sir Edwin Lutyens. The west window has notable modern glass and 25 medallions of seventeenth century German or Swiss origin which were brought from the Duke of Buckingham's private chapel at Edgware. Its chief claim to fame, though, is the fact that it dates from the Commonwealth period and only one other church shares this distinction, that of Staunton Harold in Leicestershire.

Inside the church are some interesting reminders of the past, such as the white marble memorial to Dr George Johnston who died in 1855. He was one of the founders of the Berwickshire Field Club and author of a book on the flora of the Berwick area. Round his portrait are carvings of some of the subjects of his studies. Another memorial is that of Colonel George Fenwick; he was Governor of the town, a friend of Cromwell and died in 1656. The inscription states that he was "a principal instrument of causing this church to be built. A good man is a public good." Depicted on the memorial are a pair of eagle heads and various war trophies.

The Scottish diarist, poet and scholar, reformer and divine, James Melville, is commemorated on a brass plaque in the south aisle. In 1580 he was professor of Oriental languages and Hebrew at St Andrews, but in 1584 was forced to flee to Berwick as a result of expressing his extreme Presbyterian opinions. By 1586 he was back in Fifeshire as a parish priest but still persisted in opposing the bishops with his radical views and eventually died in 1614, once more in exile at Berwick.

Another memorial to one of the town's notabilities is on a bronze plaque fixed to a statue of Hygeia in front of the infirmary. This remembers Dr Philip Whiteside Maclagen, who died in 1892, with the inscription "a noble life spent ungrudgingly in promoting the highest interests of humanity."

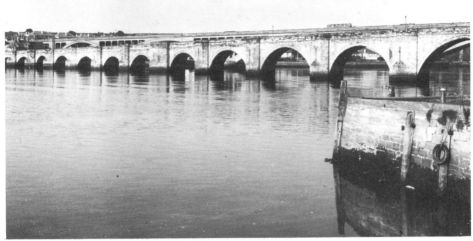

The Old Bridge at Berwick on Tweed, once proud carrier of the Great North Road.

The Town Hall in Marygate was built between 1750 and 1755 by another Master of the London Masons' Company, Samuel Worrall. It was once used as a jail and a balustrade runs round the roof where the prisoners exercised. In the eighteenth century it was described as "perhaps the most healthy and pleasant one in the kingdom, with excellent views of the town, the German Ocean, Bambro' Castle and Holy Island." Considering the general squalor in which the ordinary person existed in those days it may well have been a case of "crime does pay" for many a Berwick citizen.

The spire is 150 feet high and the lantern contains eight bells, four of which belong to Holy Trinity Church which does not possess a tower in which they could hang. These bells are rung for Sunday services at the nearby church and every weekday evening a curfew is pealed at 8.00 p.m. yet another connection with the town's historic past. Outside the Town Hall are the old stocks last used in anger in 1857 and close by are the library, museum and art gallery. The museum contains relics from the Battle of Flodden and the long red military waistcoat believed to have been worn by Charles I when he visited Berwick in June, 1633. The art gallery has works by Degas, Lavery, Opie and Raeburn in its collection.

The barracks date from about 1720 when the great Marlborough was Master of the Ordnance. They were probably designed by Sir John Vanburgh, architect of Seton Delaval Hall in the same county, and were the first barracks to be built in Britain, as a result it might be said, of public opinion, since the townsfolk had protested long and loud about the burdensome task they had to shoulder of billeting soldiers in their houses. There is a massive gate house with a pair of fine ornamental iron gates and a large coat of arms. It was until quite recently the joint depot of the Royal Scots and King's Own Scottish Borderers and is now a regimental museum.

Between the barracks and the sea is the pleasant open area known as Wallace Green, named after the great patriot. It is from here that one of the town's ancient customs is commemorated each year on the 1st May. This dates from 1438 and is known as Bounds Riding which originally was intended annually to re-define the town boundary after the truce with Scotland; the Bounds covers an area of eight square miles and forms the extreme north-east corner of England.

The town wall and barracks, Berwick on Tweed.

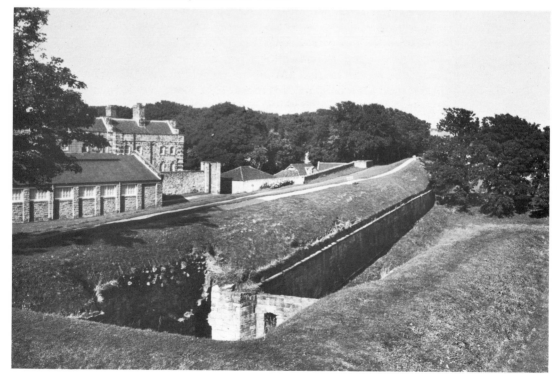

As early as 1799 there were fifty-nine public houses in the town; in addition there were three coaching inns, the *Hen and Chicken* in Sandgate, the *Red Lion* in Marygate and the *King's Arms* in Hide Hill where Dickens stayed when he gave a reading of his works in the adjoining Assembly Rooms in 1861. The inns are reminders of the stage-coach and post-horse days when Berwick held an important place on the east coast London-Edinburgh route. Another link with the past is the continuing manufacture by the Cowe family in Bridge Street of "Original Berwick Cockles", a sweetmeat beloved not only by generations of children but also by those of a more mature age.

The town wall is an impressive structure dating from Elizabethan times and there are a few remains of a much earlier wall built by Edward II and which was about two miles in length. The later structure encompasses one of the nineteen towers which formed part of Edward's wall. It is octagonal, known as the Bell Tower and was rebuilt when the Elizabethan wall was constructed. It got its name from the fact that watchmen were posted there to give warning of marauders approaching from the north and when these were observed a bell was rung and a beacon lighted. The north-east angle of the Edwardian town was marked by the erection in Mary's reign of the Lords' Mount Tower. At this point the defence work turns in a southerly direction towards the massive Brass Bastion where the Elizabethan section begins. Two Italian engineers, Contio and Portinari, were responsible for the design about 1560 and their work is the best surviving example of its kind in Europe. In front of the Bastion is a low projecting wall, known as Batardeau, which controlled the water level of the moat; the sluice grooves are still visible in the stonework. Similarly in the case of the Cow Port Gate, the only remaining original gateway, the portcullis grooves can still be seen and there is also a heavy timber door. The Windmill Bastion has underground chambers projecting from the wall line and nearby is a heavily buttressed building without windows; it resembles a church and was originally a magazine.

The Ness Gate is relatively modern, dating from 1816 and gives access to the half mile long stone breakwater or pier which was built in 1810 at a cost of £40,000 and which has at the end a 60 feet high lighthouse, the white light of which is visible for twelve miles, flashing at five second intervals. Proceeding further along the wall from Ness Gate one soon arrives at Fishers' Fort which is an emplacement distinguished by a Russian gun captured at Sebastapol during the Crimean War. This is followed by Four Gun Battery, so named because of its four stone platforms and embrasures. Canon's Tower stands at the river mouth. The Saluting Battery has 22 gun platforms of stone with a loophole in front of each.

It is appropriate that we should end our journey back at the river and at the eighteenth century Custom House; it is an outstanding example of Georgian architecture situated in Quay Walls, one of the finest streets in the town and is an important part of Berwick's maritime history of which surprisingly little is recorded. For many years it had an important whaling industry but by 1843 it had ceased to exist; also, herrings and kippers were of importance with a large export trade to the Baltic but this too has declined in recent years. One connection with this trade of a hundred and fifty years ago can be seen at 1, Wellington Terrace which has harpoon heads carved on the front door, signifying that it was built for a whaler.

Passenger traffic was important from the mid-eighteenth to mid-nineteenth centuries and coupled with this was light cargo transportation. Leith and London were the terminal points and a fast cutter known as a "Berwick Smack" was used for the purpose. These boats were quite small, accommodating no more than ten passengers but carrying cattle and horses as deck cargo. Parboiled salmon stored in tubs was a regular item of cargo. They had a large spread of canvas and fine lines and often accomplished the journey in 72 hours given favourable conditions of wind and sea. A first class ticket cost £1. 10. 0. (£1.50)., £1 was charged for steerage accommodation, 10/- (50p) for children and 5/- (25p) for a dog though one cannot imagine many of these being taken aboard at such a high percentage of the human fares. There were several famous names such as *Ann, Commerce, King William, Lively, Princess Charlotte* and *Stately*, but by 1840 these had been displaced by two of the newfangled steamboats —*Manchester* and *Rapid*. They only survived for about twenty years before themselves being displaced by three clipper schooners — *Teviot, Thames* and *Tweed*. Ultimately the railway was responsible for the elimination of the coastal traffic and the schooners were directed to the Baltic and Mediterranean trade. Through the years the owners and directors conducted their meetings in the *Hen and Chicken* and the Company was the forerunner of the Berwick Salmon Fisheries Company which came into existence in 1872.

This Company controls the salmon fishing on the river and is one of the district's major employers. The Tweed Fisheries Act, 1857 is the legislation under which the fishing is controlled. The season is from 15th February to 14th September though even during this period fishing is prohibited from noon on Saturday to Monday morning. The wear-shot net method is the only permitted and entails the net being paid out from a flat bottomed punt, misnamed a "coble", in a circular form and immediately drawn to the shore; it can be of any length providing it does not block the navigable channel and must have a mesh of not less than seven inches in circumference. Each boat is generally operated by five/seven men whose leader is called a foreman. The ceremony of crowning the Salmon Queen was revived in 1945. Originally it was a religious festival but nowadays is a popular social event held in the third week of July and includes a carnival, sports and a ball in the Corn Exchange. This ceremony emphasises the importance of the salmon fishing industry to the economy of Berwick and indeed salmon, mostly for the London market, along with grain from the agricultural hinterland comprise the town's major export trade.

It is recorded that 5,000 salmon were caught in one day in 1959 and as far back as 1842 the season's haul amounted to 14,247 salmon, 76,422 grilse and 58,261 sea-trout. Fifty square miles of open sea, an area encompassed by a five mile extent of coast to the north, five to the south and five out to sea from the land is forbidden salmon fishing territory except to the Company in due season. So far as the river is concerned above the sea fishing limit at Norham control is exercised by the Tweed Commissioners, a body composed of riparian owners of a fishing value of £30 per annum.

To a certain extent the riverside is marred by industrial development such as Fairmiles' shipyard situated on the narrow spit of land between the river and the medieval wall, by the dock area and by the Tweedmouth expansion on the south bank of the river. These factors all help to support the prosperity of the town to which tourism is a more recent contributor. To offset these aspects of commercialism there is a delightful riverside walk along New Road, past Lady's or Conqueror's Well and beneath the Royal Border Bridge, a walk as a last reminder of the glories of the river further upstream.

It is interesting to recall that the boat used by Grace Darling and her father when they went to the rescue of the *Forfarshire*, wrecked on the Farne Islands in 1838, was made in Berwick.

Tweedmouth forms part of the borough and is a large and not particularly attractive village. The new dock constructed in 1871 at a cost of £66,000 has a surface area of three to four acres with berths for sixteen vessels. Tweed House facing the bridge was formerly an important posting-house referred to by Smollett in *Humphrey Clinker*. The *Thatch House Tavern* possesses some old ladles and punch bowls reputed to have been used by men working on the construction of the bridge in the seventeenth century. When Berwick was in Scottish hands Tweedmouth served as the English base and at the point known as Hang-Dyke-Heuk Edward III in 1333 hanged Thomas, the son of Sir Alexander Seton, Governor of Berwick, when he refused to surrender the town. Tweedmouth Feast begins on the 18th July if it is a Sunday, or on the Sunday next following, and commemorates St Biosel or Boswell who was an Anglican missionary and Prior of Melrose and who died on 18th July 661. The Church was built in 1780 on the site of a Norman Chapel and possesses an eighteenth century copper weathervane of a salmon over a yard long. In the churchyard lies the body of James Stuart who died in 1844 at the reputed age of one hundred and fifteen. He was a larger than life local character known affectionately as Jimmy Strength and had the distinction of having a statue raised in his memory on Palace Green in Berwick. As his nickname implies he was renowned for his great strength and is credited, amongst his other achievements, of lifting a hay-cart weighing one and a half tons.

Journey's end; the river flows quietly into the North Sea at Tweedmouth.

Now at last the river has come to the end of its journey and flows into the sea by the lighthouse on the breakwater on the north bank and the village of Spittal on the opposite shore. Spittal is a corruption of hospital and refers to a lazar-house situated there in pre-Reformation times. Such houses were scattered all over the kingdom and the name derives from Lazarus the leper. These hospitals were shelters for the poor and handicapped and their good services were brought to an abrupt end with the dissolution of the monasteries since they were activated and administered by the Church.

Spittal is situated in the angle formed by the junction of the river mouth with the coastline and has a long stretch of fine sands and rock pools. Formerly it had an important herring fishing industry and was the haunt of smugglers. Now it is a seaside resort with amusements and sporting facilities, readily accessible to Berwick and to the beautiful, historic and romantic river which here reached its destiny with the sea nearly one hundred miles from its birthplace high in the Tweedsmuir hills above Moffat.

Bibliography

Burnett, George, *Companion to Tweed*. Methuen & Co. Ltd, 1945.

Butler, William S., *Discovering the Borders*. 1978.

Feachem, Richard, *Guide to Prehistoric Scotland*. B. T. Batsford Ltd, 1977.

Fenwick, Hubert, *Scotland's Castles*. Robert Hale Ltd, 1976.

Finlay, Ian, *The Lowlands*. B. T. Batsford Ltd, 1967.

Finlay, Ross, *Touring Scotland, The Lowlands*. G. T. Foulis & Co. Ltd, 1969.

Hammond, Reginald J. W., F.R.G.S, (ed), *Complete Scottish Lowlands*. Ward Lock Limited, 1974.

Home, Lord, *The Way the Wind Blows*. William Collins Sons & Co. Ltd, 1976.

Langley, Robert, *Walking the Scottish Border*. Robert Hale & Company, 1976.

Lea, K. J., Gordon, G. and Bowler, I. R., *A Geography of Scotland*. David & Charles (Publishers) Ltd, 1977.

Lochhead, Marion, *Portrait of The Scott Country*. Robert Hale Limited, 1968

Mackie, Euan W., *Scotland: An Archaeological Guide*. Faber and Faber Limited, 1975.

Mackie, R. L. revised by Donaldson, Gordon, *Mackie's Short History of Scotland*. Oliver & Boyd Ltd, 1962.

McIntosh, I. G. and Marshall, C. B., *The Face of Scotland*. Pergamon Press, 1970.

Mee, Arthur revised by Linnell, C. L. S., *The King's England, Northumberland*. Hodder & Stoughton, 1969.

Morton, H. V., *In Search of Scotland*. Methuen & Co. Ltd, 1945.

Morton, H. V., *In Scotland Again*. Methuen & Co. Ltd, 1945.

Preece & Wood, *The British Isles*. University Tutorial Press, 1974.

Scott, Malcolm A., *Where to go and what to do in Scotland*. Heritage Publications, 1979.

Sixsmith, E. K. G., *Douglas Haig*. Weidenfeld & Nicholson Limited, 1976.

Temple, Arthur, *Hymns We Love*. Lutterworth Press, 1954.

Tomlinson, William Weaver, *Comprehensive Guide to Northumberland*. David & Charles, 1968.

Tranter, Nigel, *Portrait of the Border Country*. Robert Hale & Co., 1972.

Booklets and pamphlets consulted and/or areas and properties visited —

Braithwaite, Michael and the Melrose Support Group of the Scottish Wildlife Trust, 1976, *The Eildon Hills*.

Howell, W. R., *Wildlife of the Border Forests of Northumberland*. Forestry Commission.

Hunt, Erica, M.A. Hons. (Hist.), *Chirnside Past And Present*, 1975.

Lang, Andrew and John, *Border Life in Days Gone By*. Macmillan Ltd, 1913 and Lang Syne Publishers, 1976.

Maxwell-Scott, Major-General Sir Walter, Bart., C.B., D.S.O., *Official Guide to Abbotsford*. 1955.

Maxwell Stuart, Peter, *Traquair House*. Jarrold & Sons Ltd, 1966.

McLaren, Calum, *Strange Tales of the Borders*. Lang Syne Publishers, 1975.

Meiklejohn, A. K. M., B.Sc., F.R.Ag.S., *The Agriculture of South-East Scotland*. The East of Scotland College of Agriculture, 1976.

Richardson, J. S., LL.D., F.S.A. Scot., and Wood, Marguerite, M.A., Ph.D., *Official Guide to Dryburgh Abbey*. H.M.S.O. 1948.

RIVER TWEED

Richardson, J. S., LL.D., F.S.A. Scot., and Wood, Marguerite, M.A., Ph.D., *Official Guide to Melrose Abbey.* H.M.S.O. 1949.

Robson, D. A., *Geology of the National Park.* Northumberland National Park and Countryside Committee.

John Buchan's Tweeddale, The Heritage Group, 1975.

Official Guide to Berwickshire, 1979.

Official Guide to Tweeddale, 1978.

Official Guide to Queen Mary's House, Jedburgh. Jedburgh Town Council, 1956.

Official Guide to Bowhill. Pilgrim Press, 1975.

Official Guide to Floors Castle. Pilgrim Press, 1979.

Official Guide to Mellerstain. Pilgrim Press, 1976.

The Financial Times.

Index